# Rosen†thal

## Excellence for All Times

Dinnerware
Accessories
Cutlery
Glass

Ann Kerr

Schiffer Publishing Ltd

4880 Lower Valley Road, Atglen, PA 19310

# Acknowledgments

The photographs and much of the descriptive information in this book come from the archives of the Rosenthal Company in Germany and from Rosenthal sales material of many years duration.

Pricing in this book has been made possible by Replacements Unlimited and the New York office of Rosenthal.

The generosity and assistance of both companies is very much appreciated.

Kerr, Ann , 1921-
    Rosenthal : excellence for all times : dinnerware, accessories, cutlery, glass / Ann Kerr.
      p. cm.
    Includes bibliographical references.
    ISBN 0-7643-0106-3 (hardcover)
    1. Rosenthal AG. 2. Porcelain, German. 3. Decorative arts--Germany. I. Title.
NK4210.R55K47    1998
738.2'0943'31--dc21        98-11207
                    CIP

Book design by Blair Loughrey
Typeset in Geometric 415 LtBT/Bernhard ModBT/Times New Roman

ISBN: 0-7643-0106-3
Printed in China

Published by Schiffer Publishing Ltd.
4880 Lower Valley Road
Atglen, PA 19310
Phone: (610) 593-1777; Fax: (610) 593-2002
E-mail: Schifferbk@aol.com
Please write for a free catalog.
This book may be purchased from the publisher.
Please include $3.95 for shipping.

Please try your bookstore first.

We are interested in hearing from authors with book ideas on related subjects.

# Contents

# Foreword

It would be incorrect to suggest that this book covers the complete production which Rosenthal has accomplished over more than a century. Such production, however finely crafted, well designed, and interesting to entertain, is far too involved to condense into one study. We will examine representative examples of the company's most interesting work, the most acclaimed lines, and those which for other reasons are important to our understanding of Rosenthal's superior position in the design, porcelain, and artistic community.

Providing the most accurate dates on these shapes and decorations has been difficult; while records often include dates of origin, it has not been possible to identify the point when older decorations were discontinued and replaced with new ones. Popular shapes were given new decorations as new artists conceived of variations, and some early lines and early decorations are still in production. We must remind ourselves that this company continues to operate and to produce new and different lines. Few other companies have been able to rival that accomplishment.

It has not been our intent to limit this study, to exclude fine work based upon age, nationality, or artist. Excellence is too wonderful to constrain in any way, save for the space which inevitably limits us. Some inclusions are very old work, others very new work. Some works have been available only on the American market, others only on the European market. A great deal of consideration has gone into the selection of works shown and the exclusion of any work should not be construed to suggest that it is of lesser importance.

# Introduction

My love affair with Rosenthal was not an innocent one. Discovering it, I knew at once that I must find room in my collection for these wonderful works. My collecting was already design oriented, but I had made a real effort to confine it to American examples. That resolve melted when I walked into a specially designed and dramatic showroom totally devoted to Rosenthal production. I searched first for information and that information came quickly. The showroom personnel gave me what sales literature they had and searched for back-dated references. They put me in touch with the New York Sales office, where the late Dr. Spiekerman sent me more material and asked the offices in Germany to send me even more. I was overwhelmed, totally lost in a beautiful world that I had not known existed. I put my reference material away for a better day, a better chance to study it and a better opportunity to share that study. My opportunity came when Schiffer Publishing asked me to consider a writing on Modernism. Such a study excited me and it was but a small step to realize that I already had in my hands wonderful information which would trace good design and the international artists who had achieved it. We agreed that the Rosenthal information would present Modernism in a product related way, an approach familiar to collectors.

As from the first, wonderful help came to me. My questions took me again to the New York office, where Jurgen Stephan, the American Sales Manager, sent me more material, fitting my project's questions into his busy schedule. Christina Norsig, who was in charge of the showroom in New York City, graciously shared her information and allowed me time to fill my mind and notebook. Robert Ganshorn, a former sales representative in Chicago, opened his files and sent them to me. He was more than generous. Sherry Lisagore, well acquainted with Rosenthal's many lines, answered my questions early and late. Chris Schapdick, who is now responsible for Rosenthal AG in this country, stepped into a new position and made room in it for my project. He has been supportive of this writing and has added to the depth of this information. Matthias Knecht, of Rosenthal's International Marketing division in Selb, was most helpful in providing a large selection of original and wonderful photographs from the Rosenthal catalogs. Many of these photographs have been reproduced here and greatly enhance the visual enjoyment of the book.

My own collection took shape as I became interested in figural pieces, but it could just as easily have developed along several other directions. As you examine the representative pieces in this book, I urge you to consider the avenues along which your own interests might develop. Accessory items are so varied that one could divide them into several categories: animals, dancers, fairytale figures, vases, and more. Dinnerware revolved around the Classic lines or Studio Lines, and it would be a challenge to collect any of these wonderful lines. It is possible to collect the works of only one artist/designer within this Rosenthal production and still have wonderful choices. Your own interests will guide you.

## Pricing Considerations

Pricing the listings presented here has been challenging. Many older shapes are still in production, having changed decorations many times. Values, in such cases, must necessarily be different from time to time, decoration to decoration. Add to that the fact that many lines, expensive when new, were not disposed of lightly and tended to become "family pieces," not discards. For this and other reasons, little has yet to come on the collector market. Since the science of pricing is less certain than all of us would like, the author has been cautious in comparing, evaluating, and attributing values. Several guiding principles were used to establish the figures which you will find here.

Foremost, pricing of items lately or still in production is not always as precise as we would like. Items purchased on the secondary market, i.e. the collectors' market, may vary significantly in price from the same items purchased on the retail market. Where it has been possible to list prices, especially in dinnerware, readers should be aware that for those items with price ranges, the lower end of that range applies to white, or the least decorated of the patterns. Where possible, we have designated decorations and priced them. The spectrum is wide, but consistent with the original price structure which Rosenthal used in its sales material.

Given the above considerations, it still was not possible to ascribe values to many items. However, the inclusion of those items was important to show documented lines, whether or not pricing was available. Where the notation "NPD" (No Price Determined) appears, the absence of a price does not mean that the item is so rare or expensive that it cannot be evaluated. It means only that an item may still be in production or that we have no exact figures upon which to rely, and to conjure inaccurate figures would detract from the presentation of the items. The exception to this is the Limited Edition Art, which is outside the experience of most collectors but is included because of its importance in Rosenthal's production.

Representative prices provided here could not have been done without the cooperation and help which was extended by Chris Schapdick of Rosenthal's New York office. He instinctively understood a collector's need to know and was quick to offer pictures and prices, extending himself to answer questions. His supportive efforts have added much to our understanding of Rosenthal's production and his ready willingness to help with pricing has added to the reliability of the values presented here.

Doug Anderson and the professionals at Replacements Ltd. were also generous with their time and effort, and their knowledge of the collector's market added immeasurably to our pricing. No other replacement firm has the depth of experience which Replacements enjoys and their consistent consideration of collector's interests is an important part of their business. Replacements is the "Who's Who" of dinnerware, and collectors, whether buying or selling, find them generous with information as well as a reliable source for long-out-of-production dinnerware and accessory items. Their suggested pricing has been important to this writing.

A parting word: this is not the last word. The collecting world, just being introduced to Rosenthal, will find much that is new here. It seems certain that there is much more. As collectors become acquainted with this production, prices will stabilize around favored lines and availability. It would seem, then, that this may be a good time to buy, a questionable time to sell. Your own judgment will be important as you establish values which apply to your collection.

# Rosenthal Excellence for All Times

Collectors who have considered excellence of design in the United States are increasingly aware of the inheritance of primary principles from the world as a whole, and it comes as no surprise that common precepts developed in England, Europe, and Scandinavia quickly found favor, influencing the work of American artists as well as American consumers. Such consideration broadens our understanding and expands our interests as we explore important contributors, major design movements, significant exhibitions, international awards, and wonderful works. It is true that, more often than not, these directions were coupled with social concerns, and what evolved as artists and designers searched for the best often caught fire and became shared precepts, common principles. Our interest has become international as we find the best of twentieth century design evolving without limits set by geography, time, place, or movement. America's own contributions to style and design have been important, but they become even more significant when they are viewed as part of the larger whole.

Sharing similar precepts, these international artists/craftsmen often worked independently, sometimes worked in groups or schools, and occasionally served as resident artists for those who would produce or distribute their work. Modernism flourished wherever it found appreciative conditions. The Rosenthal firm provided that environment.

As the nineteenth century closed, work in England by John Ruskin and William Morris established the Arts and Crafts Movement. Seeking to reform and popularize art by the production of finely designed articles to be used in everyday situations and priced affordably, these pioneers were to establish a new concept of art and its application to every-man. With such a straightforward purpose, simple in theory, they attempted to overthrow centuries of art as the due of the wealthy and extend it into the lives of those of lesser means.

As early as 1903, extensions of this concept found root in France and Belgium, where it was called Art Nouveau, in Italy, where it was called Stile Liberty, and in Scotland, where it was called the Glasgow School style. The Jugenstil in Germany and the Vienna Secession in Austria followed. These would lead to Joseph Hoffman's work with the *Weiner Werkstatte* (Vienna Workshop), an outgrowth of the earlier Vienna Secession Movement. None of these was more important than the Bauhaus founded by Walter Gropius in 1919. These workshops in England and Europe, especially those in the German speaking world, soon drew attention in The United States. Attempting to bring art, industry, and commerce into harmony with one another, and in so doing to create a more humane environment and address the social problems caused by industrialization, they searched for aesthetically pleasing designs which would be suitable for mass production. This objective became the mantra for art and design in the western world and many of design's most influential names were associated with the concept. Gropius was joined by Mies van der Rohe, Oscar Schlemmer, Paul Klee, Marcel Breuer, Wassily Kandinski, and many others. Each country, each individual, each school, each manufacturer made major contributions to the emerging styles and it was accepted that superior schools of art on the European continent were adding dimension to traditional art as it had been recognized. Americans rushed to join those whose work they admired and the work became an International Style.

From such beginnings evolved Modernism as we recognize it. Typified by uncluttered forms, simple lines, with social concerns significantly important to people of average means, it was a good beginning. Such lofty principles have often been translated but never improved upon, and are generally accepted as one of the most important social legacies of the twentieth century. The new Modernism should never be confused with Contemporary or Modernistic, but it can be said that these principles continue to influence the most skilled artists, designers, and architects of our day.

Progress and reform of design were interrupted by major world events early in the twentieth century. None were more significant than the two world wars, for they brought attacks on all the arts, direct attacks. After World War I, Europe's rebuilding expenses left little to be spent on anything but necessities. Artists could look for little in the way of government assistance, and patrons were reluctant to encourage what they considered to be questionable advances in artistic forms. Later, Hitler, a sometime house painter himself, assumed the position of art critic and prohibited all artistic work of which he did not approve. He favored almost no innovative works in any art field: painting, music, design, dance. Those whose work did not please him were forced to halt their work, which he called "Degenerative Art." Some conformed. Some, seeing no hope for their work, resorted to suicide. Others fled to the free world where they could continue to work. It would be difficult to measure the influence which these immigrant artists brought to their new homes, but they were welcomed by like-minded artists, eager to exchange ideas. Many, perhaps most, never returned to their homelands. Walter Gropius, himself, left Germany and came to the United States in 1937. With the most impressive credentials, he joined the faculty of Architecture at Harvard and taught the same subject at The Illinois Institute of Technology.

There was, of course, a great amount of anti-German feeling in the world during the war years, but to the credit of the artistic community, The Design and Industries Association's founder Clutton Brock is quoted: "Where an enemy has a noble lesson to teach, it can only be learned from him nobly." Without question, the artistic community gathered strength in spite of the divisive situation in the political field. In their search for freedom in which to work, a cohesive group of artists and designers persevered and their art flourished.

Our Rosenthal story has early roots, however, and we must look for them at the mid-mark of the nineteenth century, for the story begins at that early date. In 1858, Selb, little more than a Bavarian village whose population was supported by the weaving industry, burned completely and the population was left without livelihood, in absolute poverty. In a humane gesture, Lorenze Hutschenreuther, a weaver, himself, stepped in, attempting to sweep away the ashes and restore trade. The weaving industry, as it had been known, was in flux due to the invention of machinery and it seemed unlikely that the destitute townspeople could continue weaving. In his search, Hutschenreuther stumbled upon a deposit of kaolin, a fine quality white clay. This was not surprising since late in the eighteenth century many porcelain factories, most notably Meissen and Dresden, had been established in the area and it had become known as the German Staffordshire District, with plants owned and operated by nobility or the state. Hutschenreuther decided that his destiny and the fate of Selb would be best served by changing its primary industry to the manufacturing of china and he thus opened the first such privately owned company in the area. All concerned were pleased and the new company attracted attention from all quarters.

In 1879, Philipp Rosenthal, German born, American by choice, arrived in Selb. Rosenthal, speaking both German and English, was the head of the China and Glass department in a leading store in Detroit, and came as a buyer for his firm. That conservative occupation obscured the colorful background and interests of the twenty-four-year-old Rosenthal. Born the son of a Westphalian China merchant, his familial connections with the china industry seemed to explain his working life in 1879 but it was also

true that at seventeen he had run away from home and worked on a ship for passage to America. In the euphoria of youth and freedom he found work as a cowboy, a dishwasher, and an elevator operator, even working his way up fortune's ladder to deliver mail by horseback in Colorado. Philipp would return to unconventional adventures for fun or profit all his life. For now, however, in Selb as a china buyer, he realized that the real profits in the china business were to be made as a manufacturer, not as a salesman. He had found his niche in Selb and would produce porcelain.

Even without the experience of those at Meissen or of Hutschenreuther, Philipp was decorating dinnerware in limited amounts by 1884. Once settled, he had married, and with his young wife, Maria, rented a room in a rundown mansion, establishing both home and factory there. Maria painted the white china that Philipp bought from Hutschenreuther, selling it from house to house from a cart she pulled. Fortune seemed kind to the busy couple and, with sales promising, they were able to relocate to Ploesburg, a mile away. The going was not easy, however, and Maria died early, after having contributed much to her husband's work. In memory of her, Philipp's first complete dinner service Maria Weiss (White) was named for her. Record claims were made for its commercial success and it was said to be the biggest dinner service in the world with 156 pieces in place of the usual 98 pieces. Philipp was established and would continue his work with rapid fire success. San Souci accrued importance when the ex-Kaiser Wilhelm II allowed Philipp to copy a design from the palace of Frederick the Great at Potsdam. Moosrose (Moss Rose), decorated by important and talented artists, followed. The lines were instant commercial successes, a departure from the lavish, over decorated patterns favored by the wealthy. The ground seemed to have been established.

Philipp, the businessman, knew the value of good design and did not insist on personal involvement with it. This businessman/potter kept his attention, and what time he could afford, focused on establishing the business policies which would involve the finest designers he could employ. They would establish a design department and he would allow them the freedom to work independently. He became known as a man who knew the business end of profit and left artistic decisions to those who were acknowledged experts in that field. Lorenze Hutschenreuther and others in the industry were supportive and the firm grew rapidly, expanding its work force to include 60 people in the decorating department. By 1891 the firm had grown to employ 225 people, making it necessary to incorporate the business. Practically, Philipp needed to make money and he soon saw that expansion could best be achieved by acquiring other firms, a practice which proved to be successful over many years. By 1910, still deep in dinnerware production, Philipp saw the possibilities to be gained by establishing an art division which would produce ornamental accessory items. He began a world wide search for artists who would turn out the very best of decorative items,

Maria coffee service in White.

vases, figurines, and the like. His search led him to a group which included Wilhelm Wagenfeld, Wolfgang von Wersin, Erich Krause, and Heinrich Loffelhardt, as well as Constantin HolzerDefanti, Gerhard Schliefstein, Gustav Oppel, Grete Zschabitz and others. The work which this group produced was impressive then and remains so today. A milestone had been certainly been accomplished.

Philipp's personal concerns were not as fortunate. His Jewish blood found him out of favor with German nationalism. Some extremists had become members of his board of directors, profiting themselves while tolerating him for their own purposes. His marriage to his second wife, of undisputed "Aryan Stock," as well as his good reputation, bought him time, however, and he was not exiled until 1935. It is said that he left ten companies and five thousand employees still in operation. Philipp would have had the last word with the Nazis except that he died in exile in 1937 at the age of eighty-two. He was buried in Bozen, the center of the German-speaking part of the South Tyrol.

His life had been distinguished and unique in many ways. His openness to what was new, his curiosity and sensitivity to his times, had established collaboration with contract artists at a time when such a practice was unheard of. All this served as an inheritance to his son, his company and the world. Always interested in politics, especially as it concerned porcelain, he had, in 1898, founded the Society of Bavarian Porcelain Industries and was its

first president. Joining others, he founded the Kaiser Wilhelm Institute for Silicosis Research and in 1914 he became president of the German Export Industry. Continually advancing his interests, he promoted various trade fairs, including one in the Soviet Zone where, because of his influence, a street named after him still stands.

Philip Rosenthal Jr., with his name slightly changed from that of his father, was the son of the second Maria in Philipp's life. He was born in Berlin on October 23, 1916 and educated in France and Switzerland as well as in England, where he attended Laurence (then Exeter) College at Oxford, majoring in political science and philosophy. Exiled, because of his family, but advantaged, because of his background, he was able to travel and hoped to make an expedition to Mongolia to study the Mongolian people for his doctoral dissertation; meanwhile he would circle the globe. War was again to intrude upon the Rosenthal plans, however. Philip was an amateur pilot and when World War II broke out he joined the Scottish Air Force. He later "attached himself" to the British Foreign Office but his nationality created problems. He had applied for citizenship in 1938 but it was not granted until 1947. Frustrated, he chose to go to Paris to fight against Hitler there. He was permitted to join only the French Foreign Legion. With the collapse of France, he turned to North Africa where he joined the Sahara Company to do underground work. His choices ended there when he was sentenced to a concentration camp. After four escape attempts, he made his way to Gibraltar and then to England. Seemingly safe, he tried to become a baker's assistant and a fledgling journalist but his political interests remained important to him and he assumed the name of "Rossiter," making his rounds of POW camps, visiting German prisoners, and attempting to teach elementary principles of democracy. By drawing attention to his ideas, he was called to the English Foreign Office where, until the end of the war in Europe, he worked in the intelligence agency in an official capacity.

When World War II ended in Europe, Philip raced to his inheritance, eager to use his acquired multinational experiences and return the firm of Rosenthal to the prestigious position it had achieved prior to the war. In spite of new connections acquired from contacts during the war, he was disappointed with the reality of the situation he found upon return. While the buildings were not destroyed, the factory equipment was out of date and the buildings themselves inadequate for the position Philip hoped to achieve. Because the main plant at Selb was located very close to the Soviet zone, restoration was slow and expensive. Kaolin could still be acquired from Czechoslovakia, but the quality was no longer as fine as Philip required and he was forced to look elsewhere to maintain materials. For some time the clay came from northern Spain, a costly alternative. Other elementary materials such as coal presented production problems. New boundaries established between Eastern and Western Europe were to present trade losses that seemed overwhelming, and with the sealing off of Eastern Europe by the Russians, three important sites were lost: the important Berlin plant and two others in

Philip Rosenthal

artists to extend his art department: Tapio Wirkkala from Finland, Jean Cocteau from France, Bella Bechem from Germany, and numerous others. While their work was immediately accepted on the Continent, America seemed disinterested, probably because its own social revolution was working its way, finding its place, celebrating the Americanism of its products in directions that would lead to industrial design. Due in part to these circumstances, Rosenthal sales had hit a new low of eighteen percent of the American market. Americans, along with Italians, were credited with the leading influence in dinnerware as well as design at that time. With disappointing figures on his desk, Philip phoned New York City. He turned to Raymond Loewy, a Frenchman with an American household name who had lived in the United States long enough to understand the cultural revolution in America and who could guide him toward his desired share of the market in the United States. He flew to New York City the following day and there saw Loewy's studio with its staff of artists and designers so skilled that the work was in demand worldwide. An agreement was made. Loewy would design medium-priced dinnerware which both believed would be well received in America. Loewy would be paid on a royalty basis and qualified designers would be used to apply approved decorations upon Loewy's Form 2000 shape. At once, Rosenthal sales to America rose to second place; only Wedgwood was more favored. The Prince of porcelain had met the Master of design.

The genius of this phenomenon was the Form 2000 shape, elegant, but not traditional. Rosenthal and Loewy felt that only shapes which could be readily decorated would answer the Rosenthal problem, and the decision was made to apply this lesson to the whole of production. In so doing, the lines could be constantly renewed. The standard was set, with the firm constantly striving to achieve avant-garde shapes, formal and informal decorations.

The Rosenthal board of directors supported Philip's intention to continue using the best artists and designers from around the world, entailing the use of more new shapes, the involvement of as many fine artists as could be found producing day to day products with style and flair. The new policy, when refined, became known as the Studio Linie (Line) and dates from 1961. Rosenthal is quoted as stating "While porcelain manufacture cannot actually be classed with the plastic arts, ceramic designers must be able to make the clay follow the tendrils of their vision and flights of fancy. The dream in their minds must become the reality in porcelain. Even kiln-fired to rigidity the lines must flow. Short of that we refuse to accept." Every artist would incorporate this dream into his work. The Danish artist Bjorn Wiinblad extended this philosophy into all his work and the French painter and novelist Raymond Peynet added humor and romance to the mix. Tapio Wirkkala, considered by many to be among the world's finest artists, set standards for himself, the company, and his profession. Timo Sarpaneva joined them in 1968, bringing many honors to the production.

Czechoslovakia. The sales organization, established so carefully and trained so skillfully, was in disorder, depots lost, markets lost. The situation seemed irreparable. Philip Rosenthal was twenty-nine, lost in an inheritance turned to shambles.

As he had done in personal situations during the family exile, Philip set to work evaluating the situation, observing changes, deciding for himself which way the firm should turn. America, he decided, was the market he must develop. American sales had come to a standstill during the war years, of course, and now Philip recognized that re-establishment of this market was crucial to his concerns. Apparent causes would not explain away all of his firm's problems, however, and to his credit, he recognized and identified with the youth of the postwar years, understanding the revolution against conservatism rampant not only in Europe, but in America as well. He was aware of the relationship between art and industry and the important balance that he must try to achieve.

With this understanding, he guided the Rosenthal Board to evaluate the inventory production, and together they decided that Maria Weiss, Moosrose, and San Souci would remain in the Rosenthal line. Much of the rest of the production was considered not in keeping with the interests of current markets. Production, he considered, should follow his father's motto "from the old, take the well-tested, from the new, take the best." With his father's motto came his father's foresight and he attacked his problem with his father's approach, turning to Europe's finest

Form 2000

These and many others worked within rigid standards. By Rosenthal policy, each shape and each decoration applied to it must first be presented to a jury composed of an international team of recognized experts in ceramic design. Once approved, the design is sent to production and the artist/designer is free to work on his own until such time as he presents another work for appraisal. Only work presented by accomplished designers is entertained and only the very finest production has survived the careful scrutiny given by jurors. Always vigilant in inspection, always looking for work with promise, the committee of art and design experts who form the independent jury have the final word on Rosenthal lines. What has resulted, though of prestige quality, has been geared for the market of the day, to be used every day.

The social concepts of the Bauhaus, the Arts and Crafts Movement, and the evolving American concepts that art should be a part of the daily lives of the greatest number of people were early tenets of Philipp's personal philosophy; his son had found a way to translate those tenets into practice. But we must not leave our potter turned advocate for human rights without noting that his long life included many interests. Philipp was an avid participator in sports all his life, driving sports cars, piloting planes, climbing mountains, and running in cross country races. Until his advanced years he ran two and a half miles a day regardless of his other activities. Master achiever that he was, he believed that scheduled social activities, even small luxuries, should be planned, and not neglected by the routine of business. "Just as efficiency is one of the main tenets of his creed, so is crescendo, not diminuendo." On business trips he managed to climb Kilmanjaro as well as other peaks around the world. He died a British subject with only the work of Wedgwood exceeding his own work in sales. His perfect porcelain is still considered a bit below that of Wedgwood but his design work clearly excels all competition. He would explain that the Wedgwoods had worked for six generations while he was but a second generation potter. They remained personal friends and fierce competitors for many years and the relationship between the firms set standards for both.

The Rosenthal firm as defined by Philip Rosenthal quickly divided itself into several separate entities, with the common credo "Commodities and works of art only keep their cultural and material worth if they have been shaped from within their age—imitations never do. Therefore, we work only with artists and designers who, though they may represent different directions, feel pledged to the original of our time." Supporting the company's premier position in the table top market is a broad assortment of decorative accessories which includes classic-traditional work as well as that which is modern, avant-garde, casual, and functional.

The Classic Rose Program combines classic shapes of traditional porcelain and glass, some of which date back to the founding of the company. These shapes and the decorations on them are constantly refreshed by the incorporation of decorative elements and moods of today, each given an up-to-the-minute treatment. The Classic program is composed of dinnerware as well as decorative accessory items. These are heirloom designs, intended to be passed from one generation to another. Each item may be characterized as art in the finest definition of the term.

The Studio Line is strongly design oriented, an innovative line including sculptural items as well as more avant-garde dinner ware. These may well be considered artistic works of major artists using porcelain, glass, and cutlery upon which they apply their designs. An after dinner cup becomes a work of art in the Studio Line and more than one hundred respected international artists and designers are at work in this division, turning out significant and outstanding creations. An abbreviated listing of these would include: Roy Lichtenstein and Dorothy Hafner from the United States; Tapio Wirkkala from Finland; Bjorn Wiinblad from Denmark; Michael Boehm from Germany; Mario Bellini, Gianni Versace, as well as Fornasetti from Italy; Salvador Dali from Spain; Nina Campbell, the Designer's Guild, and Henry Moore from Great Britain; Gilbert Portanier from France; Johan van Loon from the Netherlands; and Yang from Indonesia. The list grows and changes as frequently as new and interesting artists present their designs to the jury for approval. The Studio, the work space for these artists, is set apart from the main plant "to ensure that its production does not impinge upon, conflict with, or become familiar to the general factories." It is an environment which encourages artistic freedom. When not designing items for Rosenthal, these artists work in their own studios.

The Thomas By Rosenthal Line dates from 1937 and uses high fired functional earthenware and porcelain to make informal dinnerware and assorted gift items. The division, with a casual approach, places emphasis on a wide variety of clear shapes. Not a lesser component of Rosenthal's offerings, Thomas items can be said to be informal classics of their own. The line, while important to Rosenthal's production, has never been well established on the American market.

Furniture, easy to live with, easy to work with, holds a position of its own with the same standards which are applied to fine dinnerware and art objects. The first furniture trials were made in 1960, and since 1972 the company has been producing artist-designed furniture and sculptured lamps, some in limited editions.

Cutlery studies date from 1962 and some of this work centers upon lines which accompany porcelain or earthenware patterns. Other cutlery lines are independent of the dinnerware lines but important parts of the production. Glass designs follow this same position; that is, some were designed to accompany dinnerware, others are functionally designed to be used independently.

Rosenthal's use of the term "Limited Editions" applies to the number produced and not yearly consecutive offerings. This area of interest, founded by Professor Arnold Bode, provides a forum in which leading artists, working with complete freedom, present their works in porcelain, glass, and ceramics. These world class artists change as newcomers contribute important work, but the group is consistently represented by leading artists of our time, including Elvira Bach, Sandro Chia, Lucio Fontana, Ernst Fuchs, Roy Lichentstein, Henry Moore, Marcello Morandini, Tom Wesslemann, Paul Wunderlich, and Gianni Versace. This listing has included many more and additions are made as significant work is recognized. These offerings are made in very limited numbers. Each is art in the finest definition of the term, not promoting a single school or movement, but rather, an example of art as diverse as the artists conceive it. These few-of-a kind pieces are often museum pieces.

Having described Rosenthal's "Limited Editions," it must nonetheless be noted that the company *has* issued a small amount of yearly limited edition plates. The artist Bjorn Wiinblad signed yearly Christmas plates in porcelain and glass from 1971 through 1994. He later presented a series of "Parables in Glass" with at least six motifs for only the year of issue. There are a few other examples. These are lovely plates, beautifully conceived yet outside the interest of most collectors, and must be considered as separate from the Limited Editions Line which interests us here. The demarcation is a sharp one, each appealing to different groups of collectors.

The artists and designers associated with the firm create products, but their influence extends to architecture; the very buildings which hold the manufacturing and offices of the company have in fact received recognition for architectural excellence. From the beginning, equal concern has been shown for the environment, with the firm investing considerable sums to protect and shape a healthy environment for its workers and its neighbors.

Many design awards, prizes, and honors have come to Rosenthal and these distinctions are too numerous to list. The Museum of Modern Art in New York City, The Design Center Stuttgart, Milan's Triennale—these and many other institutions of high repute have awarded tributes to the work of the company. Over 160 design prizes have been received and many pieces are in permanent museum collections.

The actual production of Rosenthal has been documented in a company *Facts* book and it is detailed, intricate, and comprehensive. To include it here would take space from the examination of product and it seems best to limit a description of manufacturing to the following: Rosenthal porcelain has a degree of hardness of 8 (the hardness of quartz), with high resistance to the scratching of cutlery, is unaffected by acids (except hydrofluoric acid), is weatherproof, and does not alter or deteriorate with age.

Obviously, highly precious porcelains with hand painting and heavy gold should be treated carefully, but other patterns are durable enough to keep their brilliance as long as the tableware can be expected to survive. Marketing practices are spelled out in the *Facts* book, and they operate under definite restrictions: another manufacturer's work may not be displayed in the same window or on the same shelf, nor may prices be reduced. The leading world market account is the United States and reflects the response to that taste, demand, and aesthetic requirements. Product selection is done individually for the North American market.

In an overview of the company's history, Philip Rosenthal credited his designers for the firm's important success: "I admit our debt to them, no one more sincerely," but adds "How many stop to think of the array of personnel who shared in the manufacture of the dinner plate set before them? Not a dozen, not a score—more like five score! The designer is only one person, working in a single capacity...The plate is the result of teamwork, of cooperation all along the line. Polished and burnished, it is only half done. It still must be displayed, sold, packaged and shipped. Each process requires its own specialist."

The Rosenthal philosophy included the use of art for daily living but it seems appropriate to add here that these beautiful wares are also "fit for a king." The showrooms of the pottery at Selb hold museum pieces and the firm's outstanding services are exhibited there. One important service was for a thousand persons and had been made to order for Ibn Saud at a cost of $125,000. Another was made for Pope Pius XII and not a single piece could be duplicated. An extremely ornate set with ornate gold decoration was made for the Shah of Persia while Soraya, his former wife, chose a simple set in white with a broad band of gold lines rayed inward from the rim. Princess Grace chose a set with gold leaf border inside a narrow gold band. Eisenhower's choice had a wide engraved gold border with the coat of arms of the Supreme Headquarters Expeditionary Allied Forces. The list goes on and includes designs fit for Xanadu and "pleasure domes" of any decree. The company has, historically, loaned examples to leading museums, allowing them to be enjoyed by all and adding emotional and living expression to masterfully executed porcelain work. We would do well, however, to remind ourselves of the principles which established the firm and which still hold to the belief that art is for everyman, whether it is found in a museum, a shop, a show, or on one's table. Rosenthal has intended this to be so from the first.

# Jurors, Artists, and Marks

## The Distinguished Jurors

The Rosenthal jury is drawn from many different fields, and each juror is considered the most qualified in his field. Given the opportunity to examine each item alone, without influence by the firm or other jurors, each is often able to make valuable suggestions or add his or her own opinions regarding the perfection of the object. Once approved by the individual juror, the design is presented to the jury as a group and only those designs which are approved by a majority of the jury are included in the Rosenthal Studio Line collection. Walter Gropius, in describing the jury process, has noted, "Collaboration is not a well meant extra, but an indispensable component of the work of industry."

For many reasons, the jury members change through the years but Rosenthal has maintained a vigilant search for replacements when openings have occurred. The following list of jury members (listed alphabetically) adds to our understanding of the exactness of expertise by which each juror is selected.

## Gerhard Bott

Dr. Bott's study of history and art history at the University of Frankfurt led him to important positions in several distinguished universities. He was the director of the Historiches Museum in Frankfurt, of the Hessisches Landmuseum in Darmstadt, and since 1975, of the Wallraf-Richarz-Museum in Cologne. In 1974 he became a member of the Administrative Board of the Germanisches Nationalmuseum in Nuremberg and was named its director in 1980. He has come to be respected as a leading expert on museums and has written extensively on that subject.

## Josine de Cressonnières

Mme. de Cressonnières studied the history of art and archeology at the Royal Museums of Belgium. She organized the "Design Center" in Brussels which remains under her management. She introduced the "Signe d'Or," a prize awarded for aesthetic industrial design and was a chief executive of the International Council of Society of Industrial Design, composed of forty-eight member societies from thirty-two countries.

## Mai Felip-Hosselbarth

A recent addition to the jury, Mrs. Hosselbarth is the current president of the International Council of Society of Industrial Design and director of the Barcelona Design Center. She has impressive credentials as a critic of contemporary design.

## Dieter Honisch

The distinguished Professor Dieter Honisch, the director of the National Gallery in Berlin, has been a professor at the Academy of Fine Arts, Berlin and the University of the Ruhr in Bochum. A member of the Association Internationale des Critques d'art he exhibited extensively in Berlin including "Trends of the Twenties." His studies have included fine art, archeology, and philosophy at the universities of Munster, Rome, and Vienna. In 1961 he received his Ph.D at Munster University and it was also there that he became president of the Westphalian Art Society, still teaching at the Munster School of Arts and Crafts. Dr. Honisch's credits are international: From 1965-1968 he was the director of the Wurttemberg Art Society in Stuttgart, followed by a position as curator of the Folkwang Museum in Essen. His exhibits have included "Forms and Color" and "Fifty Years of Bauhaus," which were shown in Stuttgart, London, Paris, Chicago, Los Angeles, Toronto, and Tokyo. He has curated many exhibitions and written many books and articles on contemporary art.

## Herbert Lindinger

Born in Austria in 1933, Lindinger studied graphic design and industrial design at the Design College in Ulm, West Germany where he was a lecturer from 1962 to 1968. A past president of the Association of German Industrial Designers, he was also a member of the governing body of the Design Council. Since 1971 he has been a professor of industrial design at the Technical University of Hanover and a frequent guest lecturer at universities in the United States.

## Lord Queensberry

At an early age while at Eton, Queensbury became interested in porcelain, never losing that first attraction. He studied at the College of Technology at North Staffordshire before devoting all his attention to the making of porcelain at Stoke-on-Trent, the important center of English porcelain manufacturing. Soon turning his attention to design, Queensbury became a critic and teacher in that area. In 1959 he became a professor at the Royal College of Art in London and head of the Department of Glass and Ceramic Design there.

## Heinz Spielmann

Dr. Spielmann, a distinguished writer on art and design as well as related topics, has published many writings. The editor of the series of publications *Epochen-Kunstler- Meisterwereke,* he has organized many international exhibitions of modern art. He is the head of the Modern Art Department of the Museum of Art and Crafts, Hamburg.

## Christian Wolters

Dr Wolters's interest as a scientist has extended his research into the art techniques of the past and their adaptation for modern usage. He has studied fine art, physics, and chemistry and was curator of the Bavarian State Gallery Collections as well as director of the Doerner Institute for the Preservation and Scientific Examination of Works of Art.

# The Artists and Designers

Working without limitation beyond that agreed upon between the artist and the company has allowed a great deal of freedom for the artists who design for Rosenthal. Internationally recognized, they present their work to a jury of competent critics. The result is exceptional, diverse, and excellent creations. The immediate review of designs and trends based upon these constantly presented contributions has the added advantage of a vibrant, ever changing, production. Unique in the industry, this policy has never allowed the company's lines to become tired, imitative, or inferior. There are artists working for the company today who have done so for decades and it seems certain that they will continue to have "works in progress," always innovative and exciting. As new artist's works are accepted, we find these additions to be examples of the most outstanding work in the decorative arts field today. Often, shapes that are old but prized are refreshed with the work of new de-

signers, again adding newness to the lines which they decorate.

The short biographical sketches presented here in alphabetical order are only a partial listing, but include many of the most important artists. There exists much interesting material, already in print, which expands upon the life, career, and production of many of these artists. Since most of these artists also did work which did not involve Rosenthal, interested readers will find that a great deal of detailed information has been documented and is easily accessible. Your public library, museum book stores, and the catalogs which accompany major art exhibits will add much to your understanding.

**Otmar Alt** was born in Germany in 1940 and represents a new style of contemporary art. His abstract art stands in the tradition of Joan Miro and Hans Arp and his avant-garde works are classics of that newness of style.

**Joannis Avramidis**, born in the USSR of Greek parents in 1922, studied in Vienna. He has been recognized internationally for his sculptural work and has taught at the Academy in Vienna.

**Herbert Bayer**, born in Austria in 1900, came to the United States after studying at the Bauhaus in Weimar. He later became a Master of the Bauhaus when it was at Dessau, but resigned in 1929 when Hitler's party in Germany declared his work to be part of what was called "Degenerate Art." A contemporary of Gropius, Bayer was one of several who arranged an exhibit of Bauhaus work in Paris in 1930. Bayer had graphic and photographic skills beyond those of many of his contemporaries and as early as 1932 was exhibiting work in the United States. He left Germany to work in the United States in 1938 and had various teaching contracts in New York. In 1946 he worked as an advisor to the Aspen Colorado Institutes and for the rest of his life he continued to be involved in the artistic world. His death came in 1985. He, together with other Masters of the Bauhaus, created a newness of design which influenced all artistic schools after that time.

**Mario Bellini**, Italian, was born in 1935 and has become known for his dramatic shapes, oversized details, and the exaggerated use of form. His work for Rosenthal expresses those interests which were important and new in the 1950s.

**Michael Boehm** was born in Germany in 1944 and studied at the Polytechnic for Applied Art in Kassel under the master Professor Arnold Bode. His travels took him to Italy where he developed an interest in work done in Murano and Venice. His own work evolved from that interest and he has become established as one of the world's foremost authorities of glass techniques used in the past as well as those in use today, developing his own creations by combining the best of the old and new. On the cutting edge of design, his work has experimented with technique

This "Galaxis" series bowl by Michael Boehm illustrates the dramatic and often labor-intensive nature of his designs. Using a "glass within glass" technique originally developed in Venice, the black glass is drawn out into a long thread and then combed into the final shape of the piece. Each bowl requires thirty minutes of time from five glass makers to complete.

as well as design, pushing possibilities into practice with results that are remarkable in both areas. Beauty is primary to his work, and his designs, often difficult to achieve, involve time and detail reserved for very important pieces.

**Rut Bryk,** Scandinavian by birth, has achieved honors in the international art community. Though first interested in graphic design, by 1939 she had turned her attention to ceramics as well as textiles. Her work has been displayed in the Victoria and Albert Museum in London, The Museum of Arts and Crafts in Zurich, and the Stedelijk Museum in Amsterdam. She joined Rosenthal in 1959 as a free-lance designer of ceramics after winning the 1951 Milan Triennale grand prize. She was also recognized in 1954 and 1958 in Cannes and Faenza.

**Nina Campbell** is considered the great designer of the Country House Style, synonymous with the "Nina Campbell Style," in which her twenty years of work has been recognized. Her work has involved a great many custom accounts— restaurants, private residences, hotels, and the like. With a unique sense of creativity and distinctive feeling for form and color, she has been the favorite designer for royalty. She has written on her own work and has won the American Fashion Award. Her style is her own and her influence on design in her time has been significant in both the United States and in Europe.

**Luigi Colani,** a German by birth, has become one of the most unconventional designers of today's international avant-garde. He was born in 1928 and studied aerodynamics at the Sorbonne, becoming an airplane engineer. From this background came his love of flowing shapes. He rejected the extremities of ideas, but willingly sought to topple traditional attitudes in search of what might be better. While his designs have been shocking to some, the body of work which he has produced show his versatility as a designer.

**Salvador Dali**, the futuristic artist of the century, was born in Spain in 1904. He developed a style of his own, admittedly influenced by his visions of the future and modern psychology *a la* Freud. His work is surrealistic, depicting dreams, fantasies, and hallucinations in great detail. By the 1930s, and at his peak, he was using biomorphic shapes in painting, furniture, telephones, and clothing. He may well be the best known of avant-garde artists; certainly he is the most controversial. His work—admired by many, derided by some—is always expensive on the art market, which he continually interests with his publicized accounts of himself. His lifestyle was as extravagant as his work, and while he called himself a "master" he continued with "My dandyism conceals my true seriousness." Dali's work, however controversial, is profound and uncompromising. By 1939, his reputation as an eccentric established, he was repudiated by the Surrealist community and came to the United States, where he stayed during World War II. After the war, he changed his work but it was never the same. He returned to Spain in 1954 where he continued to paint until he became too ill to work.

**Piero Fornasetti,** born in 1913, lived and worked in Milan until his death in 1988. His was the ability to turn decoration into an art of perfection and he accomplished wizardry of design. Although his work has been copied, he is recognized as one whose style combined the decorative elements of the Renaissance, the Rococo, and Newclassicism. His fantasies still live and the Rosenthal Classic line illustrates his ideas and their styling in illusion.

**Ernst Fuchs,** born in Austria in 1930, studied art from an early age, working in Paris for a time. He has been recognized as one of the founders of the Vienna School of Fantastical Realism. His visions have brought reality and the dream world together with great artistic intensity. His work is intense and detailed, often derived from religious or mythological themes.

**Friedrich Grasel,** born in 1927, studied at the Art Academies in Hamburg and Munich. His work involved industrial forms, with tubular shapes predominating, achieving a whole with new significance. His work was respected in the artistic community and he was awarded distinctive honors for it.

**HAP Grieshaber,** a German born in 1909, lived close to his birthplace until his death in 1981. Art, for Grieshaber, was an essential part of life, a life that he communicated with by means of his work. He developed wood-cut techniques which he applied with strong and forceful lines and he carried these skills of wood carving into his entire creative output. He was a professor at Karlsruhe Academy of Art and was awarded many distinctions for his work. His use of bold, direct strokes in his decorations are typical.

**Walter Gropius,** founder of the legendary Bauhaus, was born in Berlin in 1883. He was an important architect and one of the most important teachers of art in our time. His honors were numerous and the large number of honorary doctorate degrees which he received came from all over the world. Together with Mies van der Rohe, Le Corbusier, and Frank Lloyd Wright, he forged and influenced design in our century as no others have done. He was said to be the spiritual father of the Bauhaus and it was always his purpose to design items which were functional as well as aesthetically pleasing by the use of modern manufacturing methods, "the creation of standard types for all the practical commodities of every day use." Gropius was one of the most important initiators of industrial design. In 1934, driven from his home by the suppression of right wing political groups (including the National Socialists), he first went to England, later coming to the United States at the request of the artistic community here. A small but adequate home was built here by his friends, who were guided by one principle: nothing in the home was to be used if it could not be bought at a local lumber yard! In the United States Gropius became director of the Illinois Institute of Technology as well as a professor of architecture at Harvard University. His friends in the design community had scattered across the free world, taking the spirit of the Bauhaus with them. Wherever the doctrine was planted it took root, and others without a Bauhaus background adopted the principles. Gropius, the creative master, went on to design the Pan Am Building in New York as well as two factory designs and a glass works building for Rosenthal. His achievements, his honors, and his career deserve more attention than we can give here, but serious students of Modernism will meet and follow the path which Walter Gropius designed. He died in 1969.

**Dorothy Hafner** is clearly one of America's most important ceramic artists of our time. She lives and works in New York, drawing her inspiration from the vibrancy of the city streets. Her work is dynamic and futuristic and

her works for Rosenthal a "playful invitation to a more casual and relaxed style of dining." From her studio in New York, Hafner has designed other similarly avant-garde lines which are sold in boutiques and prestigious establishments across the country. Her interests have extended to textiles and she seems to seek out any medium upon which she can make a statement.

**O.H. Hajek,** born in Czechoslovakia in 1927, lived and taught in Stuttgart. He has been chairman of the German Artist's Federation. Recognized as an urban artist, he expressed social concerns with his work, aiming to make the environment more understandable and more humane through the use of color. He has been quoted as believing that town squares should serve as orientation points for the individual and has transformed many German town squares from monuments into art.

**Erich Hawser,** born in 1930, has worked since 1952 as a free-lance sculptor. He is one of a few German sculptors whose work has found international recognition. Using steel as his medium, he achieves surface effects of light and shade through his predominant use of sharp edges and folds.

**Raymond Loewy,** an American born in France in 1893, may well be the designer whose work and advice brought success to Rosenthal at a critical time. Loewy had been trained as an engineer, but his early work in New York was in graphic and theatrical design. By opening his own design firm in 1930, he singled out industrial design as a profession apart from studio and custom design. The amount of work with which he was associated was vast and he went on to employ hundreds of artists in many cities in the United States. It has been said that in the 1940s and '50s, an "estimated three out of every four Americans came into contact with at least one of his products each day." That influence has continued, growing from the precedents which Loewy set in his career.

**Martin Matschinsky,** born in 1921, was married to **Brigitte Denninghoff,** who was two years younger. They worked together for many years, evolving their ideas and integrating them into their work. In 1955 the couple produced large sculptures characterized by a rich surface structure. Denninghoff had been a former assistant of Henry Moore.

**Marcello Morandini,** born in 1940, is recognized as having an important place among the Constructivist artists of our times. His work in sculpture and graphics illustrate motion studies with excellence.

**Rosemonde Nairac** was born in Worcestershire, England in 1938. She studied at the Royal College of Art there and her work qualified her as an important designer. She had various creative interests, including archeology and illustration. We know her here for her decorations, which are often classically inspired, made distinctive by clean lines and bold colors.

**Eduardo Paolozzi** was born in Leith, Scotland and lived for many years in London. He studied at the Edinburgh College of Art and the Slade School in London. He has taught art in Cologne, London, and Hamburg, as well as at Berkeley in California. His work has been recognized internationally, acclaimed as an important contribution to modern art.

**Otto Piene**, born in Westphalia in 1928, lived and worked in both Düsseldorf and New York. He was a member of an inner circle of artists which were known as "Ground Zero," a group which had a great influence on contemporary art. He was a professor of environmental art at the Massachusetts Institute of Technology in Cambridge. The rainbow which was created for the closing ceremony of the 20th Olympic games in Munich was Piene's concept.

**Ambrogio Pozzi**, an important Italian designer, was also a producer of ceramic designed work. He and his brother owned a ceramic factory near Milan, where Pozzi's work was produced. He turned out a great deal of very finely designed work and is well known in the Industrial Design community. He has worked for Pierre Cardin in Paris and designed a table service for the Italian airline Alitalia. His work has won many awards, many honors for the products which he designs.

**Lord Queensbury**, born in 1929, became a professor of ceramic design at the Royal College of Art in London. He studied there as well as at the North Staffordshire College of Technology and worked for many years as a designer in the English ceramics industry. Lord Queensberry is acknowledged a connoisseur of European and Asiatic ceramic art. In 1964, joining Martin Hunt, he founded a group which was named the Queensberry-Hunt Group. His name has been added to those of other jurors who decide upon the worth of items as they are offered for inclusion in the Rosenthal Studio Line collection.

**Ivan Rabuzin**, born in 1922 in Yugoslavia, is considered one of his country's leading naive painters. Naive painting, in contrast to that which is done by those with formal, academic training, is that work in which artists spend many years painting as a hobby before devoting themselves completely to their art. By trade a carpenter, Rabuzin also ran a furniture shop before devoting himself exclusively to his painting.

**Timo Sarpaneva**, born in Helsinki in 1926, was a student of design and graphic art from his earliest days. In the 1950s his use of organic form received international recognition, bringing him an honorary doctorate from the Royal College of Art in London. In 1977 the Finnish President appointed him as Professor. Like his Scandinavian contemporaries, Sarpaneva worked in many mediums, which

included cutlery, exhibition design, graphics, metals, wood, textiles, wax, and lighting, as well as ceramics. He taught at CSI from 1953 to 1957 and for a year of that time was also the art director at a cotton mill. Those years were followed by various work for several companies, including Corning in the United States for whom he worked with plastics. Important work was done in glass design for Venini in Italy. In 1970 Sarpaneva joined Rosenthal as a free-lance artist and has added many fine works to their production. The many awards which he received reflect the variety of materials with which he worked. Those awards came to him from the Milan Triennale in 1951, 1954, 1957, and 1960. In addition, he was awarded an honorary doctorate by the Royal College of Art in 1957. In the 1960s Sarpaneva's work received attention with a full retrospective in Moscow and a display in the crypt of Helsinki Cathedral which showed how his Suomi shape was developed.

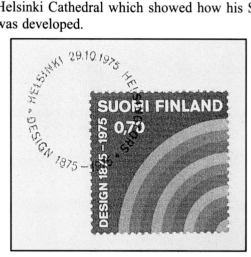

Postage stamp by Timo Sarpaneva.

Gold medal awarded to Sarpaneva for his Suomi shape. This is the Italian Republic's Presidential Gold Medal, which is given in competition for porcelain and ceramics and is the highest award given to a porcelain shape.

**Alev Siesbye** was born in Istanbul, Turkey and has lived in Copenhagen and Paris. Her works are to be seen as a contemporary continuation of the arabesques and ornamentation inherent in the design traditions of Asia Minor. Siesbye's works have achieved international recognition and are represented in the most respected museums in Europe.

**Johan van Loon**, born in Rotterdam in 1934, began his studies in textile design but turned to ceramic design in 1958. He studied at the Camberwell School of Arts and Crafts in London and the Stockholm College of Art as well as in the studios and workshops of several Dutch ceramic artists. After 1977, he was a professor of ceramic design at the St. Joost Academy of Art in Breda. His work is part of many international museums' permanent collections and has been the feature of many exhibits. He is generally recognized as one of Europe's most outstanding ceramic artists.

**Victor Vasarely**, born in 1908 in Hungary, moved to France in 1930. For many years he has ranked among the leading artists of our time, and is said to have been one of the forerunners of the Op Art movement. His position and the significance of his work are internationally acknowledged. His personal concept is that it is possible for man to find harmony in the stimulus of art and he believes it should generate pleasure and contentment. Vasarely has written several books which illustrate his vision of more colorful environments, more humane spaces in which to live. In 1976 a museum was opened in Aix-en-Provence as a living center and Foundation for his practical and theoretical works. His personal concerns for man's life and the quality which is brought to it by a more attractively designed environment are expressed there. Internationally acclaimed, Vasarely has won awards from the Milan Triennale, was given the Guggenheim Prize and the Carnegie Institute's Painting Prize, and holds an honorary doctorate given him by the Academy of Applied Arts in Budapest.

**Gianni Versacci**, Italian by birth, but internationally claimed by the fashion design and theatrical worlds, brought luxury to the Rosenthal family of excellence. Born in 1946, he achieved his important position in design early and added newness in a style unmistakably his own. His details are sumptuous, intricate and involved, his colors so important, so clearly ones which he seemed to own. Colorful in life, Versacci's work remains so.

**Alan Whittaker**, born in Lancashire in 1953, studied at the Royal College of Art in London and went on to become a professor of ceramics at St. Helen's College, Merseyside, England. After 1978 he had a studio in Moss Bank, England.

**Bjorn Wiinblad**, born in Denmark in 1919, is recognized as one of the most versatile and outstanding artists of our century. Beginning his career as a painter, he soon found his work attracting international attention. That work has extended to oil painting, metals, glass, stage and poster design, furniture, illustrations, and textiles, as well as porcelain. Recognized as a pioneer in modern design, he covers the globe, designing world wide. Throughout his work, there is a quality of joy, often extended to fantasy and the whimsical. Celebrated world wide, Wiinblad was made an "Honorary Craftsman" by the Queen of Denmark. Japanese magazines have named him as the most interesting Western designer. From 1946-1956, he did work for Nymolle, and collectors often see examples of that work, unsigned but recognizable. In 1952, he opened his own studio with Gutte Eriksen under Jacob Bang. He first joined Rosenthal's design community in 1957 and his work there has resulted in some of their finest designs.

Annual Porcelain Plate for 1977 by Victor Vasarely.

The design for this ornamental vase by Victor Vasarely appears to be almost four-dimensional, with an "exploding" front.

An example of Wiinblad's lively signature.

**Tapio Wirkkala**, was Scandinavian by birth, although most of the western world would like to claim him as their own. His legacy to the art world has been a large one, spanning a long life which began in 1915 and ended in 1985. He is celebrated as one of the finest designers of our times. Wirkkala studied at the Institute of Industrial Arts in Helsinki, graduating in 1936. Fifteen years later he was the art director there. Working to achieve aesthetically pure shapes, convincing design, and functional solutions, he chose to use detailed individual studies, fashioning them from wood in the sculptural style in which he was trained. In so doing, he felt that he could best "distinguish between the essential and the superfluous." He never leaned toward the overdone, never overworked details. Instead his use of shape is clear and precise with function and proportion as his guides.

Wirkkala has been awarded many international decorations as well as an honorary doctorate from the Royal College of Art in London. His honors, many and lavish, have included grand prizes in design, glass, wood, and sculpture. He was given the Medal of the Year at the Society of Industrial Arts in London in 1958 and two years later in Milan he was given the Gold Medal and Grand Prize. From 1951 until 1964, he won seven grand prizes in Milan as well as three Triennale exhibitions. Among his many works which have been shown are the Finnish Exhibition Pavilion at the Triennale in Milan and the very large *Ultima Thule* wood relief at the Montreal World Exhibition. Wirkkala has designed in ceramics, cutlery, exhibition design, glass, graphics, lighting, sculpture, and wood and he has been associated with the leading designers of this century, contributing to the finest production of many firms. The glass Kanttarelli vase which he did for Littala in 1947 is on permanent display at the Metropolitan Museum of Art. His glass designs for Venini, including the Coreano dish in 1970 and the Bolla vase the same year, have drawn attention to this portion of his work. By the 1950s his work had become more abstract, though he continued to express his interest in natural forms. The silver work from that period shows artistry in concept, and styles created then were later adapted in porcelain vases he designed for Rosenthal. His hanging lamps, dating from 1960, were winners of the 1960 Gold Medal in Milan. His Composition cutlery done for Rosenthal in 1963 was joined by knife made of stainless steel, polyamide, and brass from the same time span. It won him a Silver Medal in Milan in 1964. A wood platter made of plywood, 29 1/2" long, was manufactured by Soinne in Helsinki and has been pictured in many important works written on Modernism. Wirkkala's work with wood involved cutting laminates vertically, by hand, and achieving stripes of various widths with curved surfaces which brought out the beauty of the several woods. Shells and trays, bowls and tables were treated in similar fashion, allowing us to see work which is typical of his interest in forms and patterns derived from nature. He worked for Raymond Loewy from 1955-1956 and his association with Rosenthal began in 1965. His glass items for Venini date from 1965. More skilled and talented than most, he had the ability to extend his items and shapes, crossing porcelain, silver, wood, and glass designs, using the same principles in all mediums. Most of Wirkkala's work is signed and some is dated.

**Fritz Wotruba**, born in Vienna in 1907, was Austria's principal sculptor. He taught at the Vienna Academy and influenced many other sculptors who, themselves, have been recognized internationally. Wortruba looked to the human body for his inspiration and he used it as witness to the loneliness of human beings in the twentieth century. Shortly before his death, he designed reliefs for the Church of the Carmelite Order in Vienna and they are among his most important works.

**Paul Wunderlich**, a German artist born in Berlin in 1927, gave up a career as a professor of art to pursue his own talents. His work often involves costly materials, precious metals, ivory, onyx, and polished marble. Using them to create magical and mystical surrealist elements, he combines organic shapes which evolve into new entities.

**Carlo Zauli**, an Italian, was born in 1926 and studied at The Faenza Italy Institute for Ceramics. With numerous awards for excellence to his credit, he has been a member of the International Ceramics Academy in Geneva since 1970.

## Rosenthal Marks

The many marks which Rosenthal used over the long period of its production are difficult to assemble, and the complexity of the firm's marking policies makes it even more difficult to use a mark in providing the information which collectors hope to obtain. However, there are some guidelines which help as we try to bring order to these confusing back stamps.

Most Rosenthal marks are found with the name of the firm written in script, usually with a cross line dividing "Rosen" and "thal." Most of these also incorporate the use of a crown above the widest part of the dividing cross line. Typical of this practice are some of the earliest Classic line marks, which were used before the introduction of the Studio Line. These were used for many years, some never discontinued, while other, only slightly different marks were used at the same time. Early marks sometimes contain the word "Classic" while others are worded "Classic Rose." From the beginning, the incorporation of a rose was used in various ways on Classic marks. Some early marks stand out because of the elaborate qualities of the mark itself and we find these with the identifying signature inside a colored and gold surrounded oval. One very unusual mark adds the letter E to the Rosenthal name, leaving us puzzled.

The signature of an artist may or may not accompany any of these marks, either as part of the mark or on the surface of the piece. In such cases, that signature may be useful in identifying the age of a piece. If the artist's signature is found on the item, but not as part of the mark, it is likely to be an old item, for it was not customary in the nineteenth century for artists to identify their work by using their signature in the back stamp. Too often, however, that signature is not included. For example, Raymond Loewy's name appears on no Form 2000 dinnerware that we are aware of. The addition of the artist's signature as part of the back stamp or in the decoration adds to the value of an item.

The Studio Line dates from the post World War II meeting of Phillip Rosenthal and Raymond Loewy and there has been a great deal of variation in these marks as well. Certainly all Studio Line items are relatively late, but they are no less important because of that fact. Studio marks give more information, however, and include the familiar signature, adding the words "Studio Line" below the signature and cross line and crown. The inclusion of the word Germany is also to be expected. These marks often include the name of the design, sometimes the name of the shape, often the name of the shape designer, and in some cases, the signature of the designer on the underside of the item. In many cases the artist's signature may be found on the pattern itself. Rarely, but occasionally, other significant information about the decorations will be found in conjunction with the Rosenthal Studio Line mark. In the case of Scheherazade/1001 Nights, for example, we find the usual mark, the printed attribution in small gold letters "design Bjorn Wiinblad," followed by Wiinblad's signature in gold. The mark then gives us three lines of information about the opera from which the inspiration is taken:

*Orientalische Nachtmusik*
*Ouverture*
*Motiv 1*

The Thomas Line marks are fewer and very different from the signature/cross line/crown marks. The informality of the line is mirrored in the marks, which do not incorporate the signature but rather emphasize the identifying word "Thomas."

In 1891, the McKinley Tariff Act in the United States required that all marks include the name of the country of origin. While this should apply to all of the Rosenthal items described herein, there remains the possibility that some items, privately imported, will not bear the origin identification. As a rule, however, we should expect that pieces made after 1891 would include the word "Germany" in the back stamp.

The letters AG in reference to a Rosenthal item indicate that production is recent, as these letters, an abbreviation for *Aktiengesellschaft*, refer to the joint stock company which controls the firm. In 1964 the official name was more descriptive and became "Rosenthal Glass and Porcelain AG."

In acquiring other firms or in naming distributors, Rosenthal added to the size and the extent of their production. These mergers often had some influence on the back stamps used. Examples are the purchase of the Thomas & Co. Porcelain Factory in Bavaria in 1937 and the association with the Block China Company in the United States in 1952. Block remained the United States distributor for the company until 1960, operating under the name Rosenthal-Block China Co. When Rosenthal opened its own offices in New York City in 1960, the distributorship was renamed Rosenthal USA Ltd. New York, NY.

An abbreviated listing of the marks which have been found is included below. While this is not a complete list, the marks shown are representative marks, showing various treatments which were used over the years.

Early mark dating from 1897 with continuing use for many years.

Early Classic mark, believed to be the first to identify the Classic Rose line.

Early mark used on earthenware.

Mark dating from 1900. This mark suggests the redesign of the Classic Rose mark.

This mark dates from 1903, probably adopted at the time of the purchase of the factory in Kronach, Bavaria. It was used until 1956.

Originally used in 1922, this is the mark referred to in the text above. Note the variation in spelling.

This is the earliest form of the mark which was to become the refined mark covering many years. In use from 1907-1956, it is difficult to explain the spelling in this mark as well.

The refined mark which has been in continual use since 1963, used on porcelain, earthenware, and ornamental pieces. This mark is often accompanied by the signature of the artist. It is not the only mark which has been used during this time period.

Thomas mark used in 1957 on porcelain and earthenware.

1961 mark found on porcelain.

Thomas 1962 mark to identify ovenware.

1963 porcelain mark.

Classic Rose mark in use from 1969-1981. Not the exclusive mark used during that time period.

1969 early Studio Line mark used on earthenware, porcelain, and other ornamental items.

1978 Thomas mark, used on earthenware, porcelain, flameware.

Porcelain mark dating from 1979.

Contemporary Thomas mark.

## The Classic Line

Rosenthal's first production was the Classic line, or the Classic Rose line. Its central theme is elegant traditional tableware and glass items, but almost from the first, accessory items of several types were included in the Classic line.

Continually seeking to enrich the Classic dinnerware shapes which have become favorites over the years, the company has incorporated the latest methods of material processing to improve the physical properties of the line. Additionally, important shapes, some from Rosenthal's founding days, have been used more recently by artists who have designed patterns which enhance the beauty of the line, bringing a newness of style to today's table. With archival treasures in the Classic line, the company re-editions designs on a yearly basis. Some shapes lend themselves to avant-garde decorations, some express the style of the moment. What results are the best of today's patterns combined with the best of yesterday's shapes.

Glass designs and cutlery patterns to accompany old favorite shapes have been added with regularity. These table accessory selections have become popular with those who have owned Classic dinnerware for many years and important to those who are lately accumulating table services.

The adaptation of different designs on similar items has become part of the Classic line and we find various accessory items: cups, vases, plates, an assortment of holiday "Bobbles and Bells," and more, all reaching back to early production while maintaining balance by incorporating the very latest treatments. These groupings seem well conceived to please the collector in all of us, suggesting themes which we may alter or add to as new pieces are presented.

Those who have collected figural pieces will find many of them as part of the Classic line. That body of work, much of it done many years ago, is especially important to collectors. Some figurals are formal, some realistic, others whimsical. All are very precious. We have included many of the major early figurals and where it has been possible, identified the artist who designed or decorated the piece. Where documentation has been available, measurements are included. All such information is presented as it has been found, yet it must be acknowledged that the presentation of the Classic line herein is not complete; such a complex listing, with yearly additions, would be difficult to achieve.

## The Studio Line

Writing to explain his company's Studio Line, Philip Rosenthal stated that imitations of artistic work would never be of value, never gain in importance, and that only original products, born of their times, were true art: "A Gothic cathedral built in the 20th century has as little value (comparatively) as does an imitation Rembrandt."

The Studio Line, which grew out of his concepts, would be an extensive one. Early milestones include Variation by Tapio Wirkkala, Gropius Service designed by Walter Gropius, and Suomi by Timo Sarpaneva. Setting those early standards, Rosenthal never compromised the artistic excellence, never altered manufacturing quality, always achieving a superior, timeless collection, a mirror of the finest artistic concepts of our time. In spite of such standards Philip Rosenthal wrote that "We do not assume to be an arbiter of taste, to design for him (the buyer). We also, at Rosenthal, are not representing a definite style, rather, we understand our role to be that of a publisher for the many different, original and creative artists of our time." The grasp has been a long one, the influence global and the accomplishment singular in scale.

The great body of Studio Line work is illustrated by that work which embodies pure design and unlimited numbers. Some favorite Studio lines are "old designs," dating from the midpoint of the century, but they remain fresh and alive, made so by the application of new patterns which use the older, favored shapes as background for exciting new work. Other examples are up to the minute in all ways. One might find them avant-garde, perhaps "Op Art," perhaps serene, perhaps shocking. Times change and the Studio Line has made room for the casual qualities which became the sign of their time. Our study will be as inclusive of this work as documentation and space allows.

# Dinnerware

Abbreviations used in the following listings include B & B (Bread and Butter) and A.D. (After Dinner).

## Aida (Classic Line)

Aida dates from 1911 when it was created to commemorate the premier of Verdi's opera. Formally elegant, this Neo-Classical shape balances elegance with festivity and its many patterns accent its versatility. A popular line for many years, its various decorations have attracted those who look for nobility as well those who choose a less formal, more reflective table.

The many items which were part of the Aida line illustrate the importance of the design. Additional items, made in some of the decorations, add to the listing here and should include: Crescent Salad Plate, Warmer, Egg Cup, and Pickle Dish.

### Aida Decorations

Azure, Farina, Frederick the Great, Garden of Paradise, Fruit Border, Blossom Border, Tropical Dusk, Ouverture, White, Claudine, Eminence Cobalt, Ariston, Provencale.

### Aida Pearl Decorations

Ariston and Provencale.

### Acid Edged Border Decorations

Gold 5MM, Eminence Cobalt, Wide Border Cobalt, Platinum and Gold, Polished Gold 10MM, and Gold 16MM.

### Suggested Pricing for Aida

Prices shown are for white, undecorated items. Those with gold or platinum borders as well as those with cobalt and gold in combination should be valued more highly.

Other complicated patterns such as "Tropical Dusk" should fall midway in the figures below.

Dinner Plate: $35-$65
Salad Plate: $27-$45
B & B Plate: $25-$30
Tea Cup: $30-$45
Saucer: $20-$25
Coffee Cup: $35-$75
Fruit Dish: $35-$55
Rim Soup: $45-$55
Soup Tureen: $325-$550
Covered Vegetable: $225-$375
Sauceboat: $150-$215
Open Round Vegetable: $65-$130
Platter, 13": $90-$200
Platter, 15": $200-$300
Salt Shaker: $35-$50
Pepper Shaker: $35-$50
Coffee Pot: $150-$250
Tea Pot: $150-$250
Sugar Bowl: $100-$125
Creamer: $75-$100

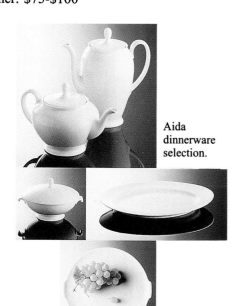

Aida dinnerware selection.

The "Tropical Dusk" decoration shown here lends an exotic touch to Aida.

The "Gold Flower" decoration on Asymmetria has an oriental flair.

## Asymmetria (Studio Line)
### Designed by Bjorn Wiinblad

In Asymmetria (#18500), Bjorn Wiinblad challenges symmetry, creating a departure in the shape of plates, lids, and handles. The complete service draws together the inside and outside edges of the plate rims with a wavelike relief repeated throughout, enhancing the geometrical effect. The motif is continued in handles and spouts. Matching stemware and flatware, also designed by Wiinblad, allow this departure in design to make a complete statement. The wave treatment is extended to the handles of the hand-blown flatware items and the crystal stems open into a swirling two-pronged base of the bowl, further suggesting a wave treatment.

Originally offered in Asymmetria "White," Asymmetria "White Gold," and Asymmetria "Cobalt Blue," the line was so well received that the decorations were extended to include "Gold Ribbon," "Gold Structure," and "Grey Structure," all conceived by Wiinblad. Indonesian artist Yang designed "Golden Orchid" on the Asymmetria shape.

### Suggested Pricing for Asymmetria

Add 50 percent for decorations which involve gold. Add 25 percent for other decorations.

Service Plate, 12": $100
Dinner Plate, 10": $50
Salad Plate, 8": $35
B & B Plate: $20
Cup & Saucer: $60
A.D. Cup & Saucer: $70
Rim Soup, 9": $40
Fruit: $40
Creamsoup Cup: $65
Creamsoup Saucer: $25
Vegetable bowl, small: $150
Vegetable bowl, large: $160
Covered Vegetable Dish, 3 pieces: $250
Sauceboat, 2 pieces: $150
Platter, 13": $150
Platter, 15": $200
Coffee Pot: $200
Tea Pot: $175
Sugar: $85
Creamer: $55
Shakers: $35 each
Cake Plate: $150
Pickle Dish: $125
Mug: $100
Egg Cup: $40
Sandwich Platter: $150
Ash Tray: $50

Asymmetria dinnerware selection.

25

## Avenue (Studio Line)
### Designed by frogskin

A late design, this service (#19200) seems appropriate as one sets an urban table in any location. Not as extensive as some lines, Avenue still contains necessary pieces for a full service line. The traditional shape departs from the ordinary in oversized handles and diagonal lines. Various designs, most of which were done in the Rosenthal Studio, feature solid colored rims in black, green, red, and yellow, as well as an unusual green/multi colored rim border named "Florence," a design by Sharon Beeden. Florence features an exotic border treatment while "Paris," a frogskin design, borders the pieces with forks or spoons marching around the border with sophistication. "New York," also a frogskin design, patterns the turquoise border in a cosmopolitan pattern. "Cairo" shows a gold band on the inner rim of the plate. Barbara Brenner created "Sydney" (sometimes referred to as Sidney) in a boldly accented random rim pattern and "Montreal," with a linear design, picks primary colors for accent. In "London," Yang has enhanced the shape with a linear theme suggestive of the 1920s on which the border print assumes a mid-position on the cup, replacing the usual brim treatment.

### Suggested Pricing for Avenue

Service Plate, 12": $125
Dinner Plate: $30-$45
Salad Plate: $20-$35
B & B Plate: $15-$25
Cup and Saucer: $40-$50
Vegetable Bowl: $35-$85
Fruit: $35-$45
Rim Soup: $40-560
Creamsoup Cup: $55-$70
Creamsoup Saucer: $30-535
Open Vegetable, Small: $115-$150
Open Vegetable, Large: $145-$165
Covered Vegetable (3 Pieces): $250-$275
Sauceboat (2 Pieces): $135-$150
Tea Pot: $135-$165
Coffee Pot: $150-$175
Platter, 13": $125-$150
Platter, 15": $175-$200
Sugar: $55-$65
Creamer: $50-$60

"New York," a frogskin design
on Avenue dinnerware.

"Sydney," by Barbara Brenner, adds color and excitement to everyday dining.

Avenue patterns, highlighting the unusual fork and spoon border on "Paris."

## *Berlin (Studio Line)*
### Designed by H. T. Baumann

"Zehlendorf" pattern.

Stravinsky's ballet is said to have inspired Bjorn Wiinblad's "Petruschka" decoration for the Berlin shape.

The form of Berlin (#80 0001) shows the designer's intention to open the shape toward the top of each item, gracefully extending the brim in a slightly flared treatment. It was awarded the Dutch design prize for good design.

Conceived as a plain undecorated line, Berlin was adapted to design by Rosenthal's own Studio as "Ascot," with a gold treatment, or "Friedrichstrasse," with a platinum border. The studio also decorated the line with a "Zehlendorf" pattern, which featured a bold colorful decoration in a lively floral treatment. "Morawa" decoration was done by Ivan Rabuzin who chose a stylized representation of the Morawa region of Yugoslavia, adding soft colored nuances and wide irregular borders to the items. Bjorn Wiinblad's "Petruschka" is the most exuberant, complex, and colorful of the decorations. Said to have been inspired by Stravinsky's ballet, "Petruschka" does have lilting, musical lines, not sophisticated, but fanciful, intricate, and involved. Lord Queensbury designed a self decorated pattern in "Queensberry Marble" on the Berlin shape.

### Suggested Pricing for Berlin

"Petruschka" and "Queensberry Marble" should be double the pricing shown here.

Dinner Plate: $40-$50
Salad Plate: $25-$30
B & B Plate: $20-$24
Cup and Saucer: $55-$70
Vegetable Bowl: $90-$120
Platter: $130-$170

"Ascot" decoration on Berlin features a gold border.

## Nina Campbell (Classic Line)

Six designs by Nina Campbell illustrate classic beauty with an updated look. "Belgravia" draws upon Campbell's favorite strong colors, with emphasis upon red. It's crewel-like floral pattern is inviting and comfortable. Her "Bloomsbury" features the English country rose on a yellow background, while "Kensington" captures the entire garden. "Chelsea," with a Baroque statement, adds elegance to informality. "Mayfair," in a blue seldom seen, is a distinctly English pattern with elaborate green detailing and "Regent's Park," decorating a red tea set, recalls the animals and pleasures of childhood. There are other wonderful Campbell designs, all late, but all very important if we are to view the scope of Rosenthal's work as it reflects traditional themes by today's foremost designers.

A selection of dinnerware pieces in Nina Campbell's "Kensington" design.

Whimsical "Regent's Park," another Campbell design, features a cheerful merry-go-round theme with colorful animals.

"Belgravia."

## Century (Studio Line)
### Designed by Tapio Wirkkala

In celebration of Rosenthal's 100th anniversary, Tapio Wirkkala combined art and technique in a porcelain that is 30 percent more translucent than any other dinnerware service. Century (#18400) was originally conceived in solid white, with a smooth but slightly suggested diamond self-pattern said to have been inspired by the sea urchin. The line challenged Wirkkala and he decorated it with "Blue Flower," a subtly colored tone-on tone decoration. The pattern, a stylized natural floral treatment, makes a romantic statement. "Century Gold" added an unobtrusive gold ornamentation with three fine border lines of varying design which do not detract from the translucency of the porcelain. "Gold" was done by Erich Demel. "Perlband," a decoration by the Rosenthal Studio, added a delicate border pattern which embellished the edges of the important pieces in glistening shades of pearly grey dots. Pearlized handles accented this subdued decoration. Barbara Brenner created the decoration "Toscana" on the Century shape; the sketchiness seen in this decoration reflects the character of the Tuscan countryside while preserving the translucency and lightness of the porcelain.

"Kontour," another Studio treatment, is a border pattern which emphasizes the shapes of the pieces, adding severity to the service. Rut Bryk decorated Century with an "Aquarius" pattern which suggests seawaves gently lapping against the porcelain, accomplishing a romantic feeling easily suiting itself to informal usage. Rut Bryk also decorated this line with "Cumulus," a white-on-white cloud pattern almost intangible against the self-pattern detail. Adding interest, clouds differ on each piece. "Helios," another Bryk decoration, uses a golden sun, created by the use of a fine gold-dust, creating the impression of light and warmth. Gold handles add to the effect of the sun's rays. America's own Dorothy Hafner's "New Wave" decoration accents the borders with the style and flair which always accompany her work, and in this decoration she blends abstractly patterned waves with geometrically accented spaces suggestive of even more waves. G. Muller-Behrendt accented Century with her "Blossom Dream," a pastel floral decoration which did not involve the border, placing the design in variant and pleasing positions.

Working with the Danish designer K.G. Hansen, Wirkkala designed a cutlery group to accompany Century. With polished silver metal parts and porcelain handles which are said to be unbreakable, the cutlery is described as dishwasher-safe. Michael Boehm, the German glass designer fashioned a series of mouth-blown drinking glasses in lead crystal to match Century. The extremely long slender stems of the glasses ease the grip as they add interest, and the sparkling ornamentation compliments the porcelain. Wirkkala also designed a companion glass service which consisted of bowls and plates in an all-over dot texture.

### Suggested Pricing for Century

Add 100 percent for decorations which involve gold, 50 percent for others.

Service Plate: $150
Dinner Plate, 10 1/4": $100
Salad Plate, 8": $60
B & B Plate: $50
Cup & Saucer: $50-$75
A.D. Cup & Saucer: $50-$85
Fruit: $45
Coupe Soup, 6 3/4": $85
Creamsoup Cup: $65
Creamsoup Saucer: $30
Open Vegetable, small: $150
Open Vegetable, large: $175
Platter, 13" oval: $150
Platter, 15" oval: $175
Covered Vegetable Dish, 3 pieces: $355
Sauceboat, 2 pieces: $300
Coffee Pot: $250
Tea Pot: $250
Warmer: $70
Sugar: $75
Creamer: $60

The Century shape in original white.

"Toscana" decoration on Century.

29

Rut Bryk created three decorations for Century. Shown here are her "Cumulus," "Helios," and "Aquarius."

"New Wave" decoration on Century.

## Cupola (Studio Line)
### Designed by Mario Bellini

Bellini's Cupola (#18600), futuristic in spirit, combines clarity of line and unconventional shapes, bringing form and function together in ways few other Italian designers had achieved. The brilliantly executed handles and domed covers as well as the self-patterned relief of flat pieces resulted in an avant-garde work typical of the sort of architectural designs for which Rosenthal had become known. Recognizing the importance of Italian influence, the Studio Line gave it a prominent position with the issue of Cupola. It became a large and complete porcelain line and was accompanied by stemware which was both bold and sophisticated, a marriage of elegance. Both the porcelain and the glass have been described as being based upon simple geometrical elements: the circle, the sphere, and the cone.

Originally produced in solid white as well as a white which contrasted with a solid black and named, appropriately, "Black and White," Cupola was later decorated by the Indonesian artist Yang, who used geometrical patterns, enhancing the design. "Strada" combined black and white lines with a band of grey, combining bold lines and spaced squares. "Nera," also a Yang concept, used bold lines, accentuated with gold squares at the key geometrical points of the pieces. Yang's "Quadratoh," another geometrical pattern, involved double black lines and gold squares, emphasizing the shape in a different way. The designer G. Muller-Behrendt adapted a bold and colorful floral border and named it "Fiorella." Brigitte Doege brings the glory of a morning sun on cool water with an almost scenic decoration named "Aquarello." A late treatment of Cupola was called "Cupola Gourmet" and involved a large ensemble of multipurpose microwave and ovenproof pieces, a series of glass dishes, and platters with wood inlays. Stemware designed by Bellini and Michael Boehm is recognized by its double stem, a departure in crystal, but a fitting accompaniment to this outstanding dinnerware.

### Suggested Pricing for Cupola

Add 75-100 percent for decorations.

Service Plate: $200
Dinner Plate, 10 1/2": $125
Salad Plate, 8": $55
B & B Plate: $28
Cup & Saucer: $75
A.D. Cup & Saucer: $100
Fruit: $45
Rim Soup, 9": $55
Creamsoup Cup: $115
Creamsoup Saucer: $30

Open Vegetable, 7": $150
Open Vegetable, 8 1/2": $175
Covered Vegetable: $450
Platter, 13 3/4" oval: $125
Platter, 14 1/2" oval: $150
Sauceboat, 2 pieces: $215
Coffee Pot: $200
Tea Pot: $200
Warmer: $110
Sugar: $75
Creamer: $65
Shakers: $35 each

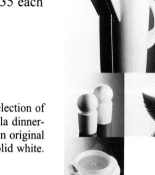

Selection of Cupola dinnerware in original solid white.

A striking geometric pattern on Cupola; this one, by Yang, is called "Nera."

Cupola's Italian origins are evident in this sophisticated table setting.

Assortment of pieces from the "Cupola Gourmet" ensemble.

## Donatello (Classic Line)

An early line, first produced in 1904, Donatello continues to be a popular design. With a suggestion of Art Nouveau, its perfect proportion combined with the unique shape of its handles adds interest to its unadorned shape. Complementing the aristocratic formality of the shape, the delicate patterns, many of which have naturalistic themes, add to its formal statement. "Sais," one of the most interesting, traces themes expressed in Egyptian mythology. An early fruit pattern of blue cherries with green and blue leaves was produced in a breakfast set only marked *Pate sur pate Bavaria*. The set included a 9 1/2" Coffee Pot, Sugar, Coffee cup and Saucer, Bouillon Cup and Saucer, Demi Cup and Saucer, 8" Plate, 12" Service Tray, and 7 1/2" Service Tray. This small set was designed by Julius V. Guldbrandson. Another early decoration by Telle Schriftzugmarke is composed of a border pattern with vertical trailing typical of the Art Nouveau of the times. This pattern consisted of a 7 5/8" Plate, 10 3/4" Platter, Creamer, Coffee Cup and Saucer, Covered Butter Dish, and Covered Marmalade. It dates from 1905-1906. Other early Donatello patterns include a breakfast set called "Rosenkavalier," by Carl Anhauser and made in 1910, another leaf pattern by Julius Guldbrandson, as well as an Art Nouveau pattern decoration with linear decoration. All these date from about the same time. Additional pieces, part of some of the later decorations, included a Warmer, Egg Cup, Dessert Service and several Vases.

### Donatello Decorations

Alcazar, Lorenzo, Carrara, Gold Staffage, Pixie, Rose D'Or, Sais, Amaryllis, Fruit

### Suggested Pricing for Donatello

Prices given are for white, undecorated items. Those items with gold trim should be double the listed price. Decorated patterns should be approximately 50 percent higher than those shown here.

Dinner Plate, 10 1/4": $50
Salad Plate, 7 1/2: $40
B & B Plate, 5 3/4": $20
Tea Cup, 6 oz.: $30
Saucer: $20
Coffee Cup, 7 oz.: $50
Saucer: $18
A.D. Cup, 4 oz.: $25-$50
A.D. Saucer: $18
Rim Soup, 8 1/4": $40
Fruit, 4 3/4": $35
Creamsoup Cup, 8 1/2 oz.: $45
Creamsoup Saucer: $20
Tureen, 90 oz.: $500
Covered Vegetable, 60 oz.: $300
Sauceboat, 13 oz.: $150
Open Vegetable, 66 oz.: $80
Open Vegetable, 42 oz.: $100
Cake Plate: $165
Sandwich Tray: $110
Oval Platter, 15": $200
Oval Platter, 13": $150
Salt Shaker: $35
Pepper Shaker: $35
Coffeepot, 47 oz.: $150
Tea Pot, 37 oz.: $150
Sugar Bowl, 9 oz.: $75
Creamer, 8 oz.: $55
Covered Butter Dish: $165
Tort Platter: $150

Selection of Donatello dinnerware.

The "Sais" decoration on Donatello features themes from Egyptian mythology.

"Carrara" decoration on Donatello sets an elegant table.

## Duo (Studio Line)
### Designed by Ambrogio Pozzi

Duo (#80 001), a dinnerware both graceful and balanced, was designed by the Italian designer Ambrogio Pozzi. Its well proportioned pieces made it an attractive background upon which many artists applied decorations. As was customary, Pozzi designed the service in white; seen with no decoration, it makes a strong statement for the fluid shapes and artful handles. Rosemonde Nairac, the English designer, created a formal pattern involving geometrical lines and circles in beige and brown. The decoration was named "Duo Baltic." "Duo Static Gold" was a Rosenthal application of a gold band which follows the circumference of the pieces. "Duo Poetic," also a treatment by the Rosenthal studio, used a grey band edged with platinum to make a similarly refined statement. Bjorn Wiinblad applied a fanciful stylized floral decoration to Duo and named it "Duo Ornamentic." Rich in ornamentation, it is characteristic of Wiinblad's contemporary designs. "Duo Bouquet" was a decoration by Wolf Bauer. "Bouquet" takes a wide border of flowers and grass in muted tones, touched with a bit of gold, and places it, interestingly, in a mid-position, allowing the shape to be the important ingredient. Erich Demel's decoration "Duo Graphic" uses a subtle beige band, once again placed in an interesting position, leaving the shape to make the statement it deserves. No other decoration is more lovely than that done by the Indian artist Srivastava Narendra. He named it "Duo Indian Rice" and drew sheaves of rice bent by the wind. The lines of the shape are borrowed by the rice stems and the curves seem to blend with the perfectly suited decoration. A bolder decoration was that done by HAP Grieshaber who called it "Pastorale." Using only black and white combined with a good bit of platinum, Grieshaber has achieved pastoral scenes which are seen as festive. Boxes and vases were also decorated with the "Pastorale" decoration. A very interesting decoration on Duo was accomplished by Victor Vasarely, who named this decoration "Manipur." Typical of Vasarely's work, Op Art impressions are used to form gradually converging parallel lines, differing on each item of the service. Evoking recollections of India's temples and palaces, the rich gold, used in a nontraditional manner, seems to approach the Duo shape using a distinctly different, more contemporary treatment. Boxes and vases were similarly decorated. The stainless steel "Amboss," designed by Helmut Alder, complemented Duo's lines. Glass to accompany these Duo patterns was named "Smooth;" the wide circumference of the bowls followed the rounded lines of the porcelain.

### Suggested Pricing for Duo

The lower range of the following prices is for White. The highest range applies to "Manipur," while "Poetic," "Ornamentic," and "Pastorale" should be considered as mid-range.

Dinner Plate: $32-$65
Salad Plate: $21-$43
B & B Plate: $16-$32
Cup & Saucer: $45-$93
Vegetable Bowl: $80-$162
Platter: $114-$230

"Duo Static Gold"

"Duo Baltic," a geometrical pattern designed by Rosemonde Nairac.

Striking and contemporary, this "Manipur" decoration on Duo was designed by well-known artist Victor Vasarely.

## Flash (Studio Line)
### Designed by Dorothy Hafner

No design speaks to Americans with a more contemporary voice than does Flash (#24500). With vivid shades of pink, purple, blue, red, and yellow, captured within a bold geometric pattern and set on dynamic shapes, Flash is eye-catching and dramatic whether in a table setting or in individual pieces. Described as Dorothy Hafner's embodiment of New York impressions, this avant-garde dinnerware brings informality to Rosenthal. Made to be used any time, any place, the colorful design differs from piece to piece. It is literally an explosion of color, a fermentation of art on ceramic shapes, uniquely Hafner's own statement. Vibrant and provocative, festive and joyful, the design is equally important to our understanding of the best of ceramic dinnerware design done in the United States during our time. It is included here, despite the fact that it is a very late design, for it seems that Rosenthal's production could never be complete without its inclusion.

Having expressed New York in Flash (sometimes referred to as Flash One), Hafner used the same shapes, adapting them to a turquoise background boldly accented with a black and turquoise alternating geometrical pattern and called it "Frisco," or "Flash Frisco." "Flash Marking" on the same shape is a more subdued decoration, bowing to the use of pastels on an up-to-the-minute pattern but preserving the newness of decoration for which Dorothy Hafner has become known. While these lines are playful additions to our table culture and should be given hand care, they are said to be dishwasher safe, thus making a complete twentieth century statement. While these patterns have been made in a large line, those who know Hafner's work best have long recognized that her pieces can be used individually as objects d'art or as an extravagant gift item. "Mars Landing," designed especially as gift items, ashtrays, vases, fruit bowls, and covered boxes expresses the decorative accessory aspect of Flash.

Flash, designed by American Dorothy Hafner, embodies the vibrancy, color, and intensity of big-city life.

Additional pieces of Flash dinnerware, shown in the "Flash One" pattern.

### Suggested Pricing for Flash

Dinner Plate: $75
Salad/Dessert Plate: $65
B & B Plate: $45
Cup: $50
Saucer: $30
Coupe Soup: $75
Mug: $65
Bowl, 6": $85
Fruit Bowl, 5 oz.: $65

Bowl, 3 1/2": $65
Bowl, 7 1/2": $175
Bowl, 8 1/4": $200
Covered Casserole/Server: $350
Gravy Boat with Stand: $175
Oblong Bowl/Baker: $200
Fruit Bowl, 1 1/2": $175
Platter, 9 1/2": $115
Platter, 14": $225
Platter 17 1/4": $250
Cake Plate, 14": $165

Carafe: $175
Shakers: $125
Coffee Pot: $300
Tea Pot: $300
Tea Warmer: $100
Coffee Warmer: $100
Sugar: $85
Creamer: $75
A.D. Cup: $40-$80
A.D. Saucer: $25

## Form 2000 (Classic Line)

Modeled by R. Latham and Raymond Loewy, this timeless design was originally produced to win the American market for Rosenthal. It served that purpose in 1954 when it was said to be the most significant tabletop design of the 1950s. Its appeal for Americans continued for many years and collectors will recognize the qualities which make it significant. Its smoothly tapered shapes narrow for interest with a high conical or tapered foot. Well-rounded handles, large and graceful with pointed knobs or grips, identify the serving pieces. The Stew Bowl is round, with no foot, intended to be used with a refined steel holder. The cover is recessed for a ladle. Both the bowl and holder are signed.

Over many years of production, Form 2000 shapes were used by the important artists as an avant-garde shape on which their designs were reflected with no shape detail as contrast.

### Form 2000 Decorations

White, Classic Gold (Border Band), Shadow Rose, Gallo Blue (Iridescent Border), Paradise Taupe, Autumn Leaves, Parisian Spring, Ceres, Rondo, Barbara, Botanique, Triennale. Other patterns may be found and the item list is larger than the abbreviated one shown here.

### Suggested Pricing for Form 2000

White is represented by the lower end of the range, "Paradise Taupe" is at the higher end. Other, more complicated designs may be valued according to their complexity.

Dinner Plate: $35-$65
Salad Plate: $25-$45
B & B Plate: $35-$65
Cup and Saucer: $50-$75
Vegetable Bowl: $85-$160
Platter: $125-$230

This Form 2000 Stew Bowl with steel holder provides a stylish way to serve even ordinary foods.

"Gallo Blue" decoration on Form 2000 has a blue and gold iridescent border.

## Grace (Classic Line)

A beautifully shaped line distinguished by a "Pearl White" finish upon which brilliant decorations are presented. Radiating romanticism, the shapes are soft with large, graceful and functional handles. The uncluttered lines make the undecorated pieces graceful and serene. Grace, with its beautiful patterns, can be beautiful on either formal or informal tables. Accessory items to accompany Grace included vases in three sizes (6", 7", and 9").

### Grace Decorations

Ritz, Africaine, Glory, Society, Royal Garden.

### Suggested Pricing for Grace

Prices given are for white, undecorated items. Decorated patterns should be about 50 percent higher than those shown here.

Dinner Plate, 10 1/2": $50
Salad Plate, 7 1/2": $45
B & B Plate, 5 3/4": $22
Tea Cup, 6 oz.: $35
Saucer: $20
A.D. Cup, 4 oz.: $40
A.D. Saucer: $20
Rim Soup, 8 1/4": $40
Fruit, 4 3/4": $32
Creamsoup Cup, 8 1/2 oz.: $45
Creamsoup Saucer: $20
Tureen, 90 oz.: $300
Covered Vegetable, 60 oz.: $225
Sauceboat, 13 oz.: $110
Open Vegetable, 8": $110
Open Vegetable, 10": $125
Oval Platter, 15": $150
Oval Platter, 13": $125
Salt Shaker: $22
Pepper Shaker: $22
Coffeepot, 47 oz.: $165
Tea Pot, 37 oz.: $150
Sugar Bowl, 9 oz.: $60
Creamer, 8 oz.: $50

"Royal Garden" on Grace evokes an informal but distinctly English ambience.

Bright yellow cheetahs join the dinner guests in this unusual decoration known as "Africaine."

Two additional Grace decorations. "Ritz" on the left, "Glory" on the right.

This sophisticated table setting features "Society" decoration on Grace.

## Il Faro (Studio Line)
**Designed by Aldo Rossi**

A small but important coffee and dinner service designed by famous Italian architect Aldo Rossi, Il Faro (#19400) combines porcelain and crystal, accomplishing shapes that are reminiscent of buildings themselves. Rossi designed the line in a handsome white, but its variations are so well suited that they seem equally interesting. "Fanale," with a measure of imagination, will suggest a lighthouse. Its red and blue lines are nautical decorations on the architectural shapes, all maritime inspired. "Cabines" decoration lines beach houses around a blue border, clearly with the skill of an architect. Rossi also decorated "Dorico," the most formal of the decorations. Yang created "Finestra" on this shape, using black squares of descending size on the border. Il Faro is a striking dinner set, but its individual, avant-garde styled items are well suited as individual gift items as well.

**Suggested Pricing for Il Faro**

Add 25 percent for Fanale, 100 percent for other decorations.

Dinner Plate, 10 1/2": $65
Salad Plate, 8": $50
B & B Plate: $25
Cup and Saucer, high: $75
A.D. Cup and Saucer, low: $80
Rim Soup, 9": $60
Fruit, 4 3/4": $50
Creamsoup Cup: $60
Creamsoup Saucer: $20
Vegetable Bowl, small: $150
Vegetable Bowl, medium: $160
Vegetable Bowl, large: $200
Sauceboat, 2 pieces: $150
Platter, 13 1/4": $125
Platter, 15": $150
Coffee Pot: $185
Tea Pot: $185
Sugar, round: $100
Sugar, square: $100
Creamer, round: $80
Creamer, square: $80
Shakers: $75
Cake Plate, 12 1/2": $100-$150

The jaunty, nautically inspired "Fanale" decoration makes a striking statement on Il Faro.

Yang designed "Finestra"
for the Il Faro line.

"Dorico" decoration on Il Faro.

"Cabine" decoration on Il Faro.

## Kaari (Studio Line)
### Designed by Timo Sarpaneva

The popular Kaari line (#226001), allows us to see the sculptural quality which is characteristic of Timo Sarpaneva's work. Soft, flowing lines extended by the high arched handle gives the design its name: Kaari translates as "arch" in Finnish. This arched handle was difficult to accomplish and the changes in firing called for careful control to prevent the handle from sagging. That accomplished, we find that the handles balances the bases perfectly, both in size and shape.

The design team of Ursula and Karl Scheid of Germany, who had won prizes in Europe as well as the "Award of Excellence" in Washington, served as glaze consultants on Kaari in its early stages of design development and Kaari's workshop appearance, seldom found in dinnerware, was accomplished through the Scheid's research. It was also possible for them to extend the line by developing bowls and vases to accompany the line. Tapio Wirkkala designed the stainless steel "Kurve" to complement Kaari. Michael Boehm accented Kaari with a glass pattern which he called "Cordon." Its outstanding feature is its heavy and massive proportions. The outside rim is frosted, adding unexpected texture to the glass design.

Several of the world's finest artists chose Kaari as the ceramic canvas upon which they worked their art. "Kaari Gray," a Rosenthal Studio design, is restrained, allowing the sculptural qualities to show to its best advantage, set off by a fine blue line. "Kaari Brown," and "Kaari Blue" were both concepts developed by the Scheids. The rich

Brown emphasized the rustic character of the earthenware ceramic and the shape combined in this way formed a harmonious whole, the dark and steely Blue only slightly less so. "Kaari Brazil," also a Studio pattern, contrasts beige and brown on some of the same pieces, while other items are accented by the use of one or the other color, again allowing the shape to dominate the design. A floral design, "Kaari Jardin," by Alain Le Foll, is an outstanding motif, large, well balanced by the shape. Bjorn Wiinblad's genius adds ornamental gold in a oversized dotted scroll application on brown, achieving elegance beyond expectation in earthenware. He called it "Kaari Gold" and it has been an important addition to the decorations.

### Suggested Pricing for Kaari

Dinner Plate: $40-$50
Salad Plate: $25-$30
B & B Plate: $20-$24
Cup and Saucer: $55-$70
Vegetable Bowl: $95-$120
Platter: $140-$170

"Kaari Gold," by Bjorn Wiinblad.

"Kaari Brown"

Teapot in "Kaari Jardin."

41

## Lotus (Studio Line)
### Designed by Bjorn Wiinblad

Lotus, a self-patterned full service by Bjorn Wiinblad, reflects the lotus leaf as it encircles the items, beautiful in the solid white in which it originally was conceived, even more interesting in the colors in which it was subsequently decorated. "Lotus Secunda Platinum," a Rosenthal Studio decoration, accented the white with a fine silver line at the brim of the porcelain. This is the only decoration for which Wiinblad was not responsible. "Lotus Blue," a pastel cobalt, added a colored lotus leaf rim treatment. "Lotus Gravada" treats the shape in much the same way, substituting a warm pastel rose for the blue. "Pastel" softens the "Lotus Blue" to a shade less intense. "Lotus Jade" achieves serenity with a rhythmic ornamental treatment, superimposing the color on the relief. In so doing, the lotus leaf seems to provide the important contrast against the jade color. In "Lotus Pergola," summer plants and vines are entwined, the color winding playfully around the lotus leaf relief. "Lotus Gold Silhouette" outlines each leaf with gold, leading the eye to the relief designs, extending the gold to accent the lotus leaf.

This line was accompanied by cutlery; the wide lotus leaf at the handle end left room there for engraved initials. It was available in sterling silver, silver plate, and gold plate. Wiinblad collaborated with K. G. Hansen in its design. Hansen designed glasses which also reflect the lotus theme, with the bowl base developed into a full lotus bloom. Their delicacy and the repeated lotus blossom make them beautiful accessories.

### Suggested Pricing for Lotus

Dinner Plate: $37-$47
Salad Plate: $20-$30
B & B Plate: $15-$22
Cup and Saucer: $40-$65
Vegetable Bowl: $80-$115
Platter: $110-$160

Dinnerware assortment in "Lotus Gold Silhouette," shown with the Lotus design spoon in gold plate.

Selection of "Lotus Blue." Note the matching glassware with the Lotus design at the base of the bowl.

Coffee Cup in "Lotus Gravada."

"Lotus Jade"

## Magic Flute (Studio Line)
### Designed by Bjorn Wiinblad

"Poetry in porcelain" Rosenthal's advertising for this line claimed, and they were close to the truth. Wiinblad, an opera lover, designed Magic Flute (#11260) with such care that this difficult and intricate dinnerware is, unmistakably, a love song. Every piece depicts a different scene from Mozart's greatest composition and on the reverse side of each plate, the libretto of the scene is handwritten in gold by the artist himself.

Not a large line, Magic Flute still answered all the demands of a formal table and was available in solid white with a generously wide border as well as a treatment which used black pieces contrasting with white. Magic Flute's elegant shape incorporated the perfectly adapted decorations placed on it. The lavish gold-treated Wiinblad decoration was named "Sarastro," while a lighter gold treatment was called "Monostatos" and one in which detailing highlighted the figural motif was named "Osiris." All were by Wiinblad. A stemware line to accompany Magic Flute was equally elegant, designed with golden dancers on the base, rhythmic swirls on the bowls.

Intricacy is a hallmark of Magic Flute's "Osiris" decoration.

### Suggested Pricing for Magic Flute

Dinner Plate: $230-$550
Salad/Dessert Plate: $120-$300
B & B Plate: $100-$250
Cup: $50 (White only)
Saucer: $95-$225
Fruit: $120-$275
Creamsoup Cup (White Only): $55
Creamsoup Saucer: $110-$275
Open Vegetable, 7": $350-$480
Open Vegetable, 8": $275-$525
Open Vegetable, 9": $295-$695
Covered Vegetable: $295-$625
Covered Sauceboat & Stand: $295-$575
Platter, 13": $375-$850
Platter, 15": $495-$1,395
Coffee Pot: $225-$426
A.D. Coffee Pot: $195-$325
Tea Pot: $225-$425
Creamer (White Only): $50
A.D. Creamer (White Only) : $50
Covered Sugar: $110-$195
A.D. Sugar: $95-$150
Stand for Sugar & Creamer: $295-$875
Stand for A.D. Sugar & Creamer: $275-$675
A.D. Cup: $40 (White Only)
A.D. Saucer: $80-$225

Selection of Magic Flute dinnerware in White.

43

Wiinblad's "Sarastro" decoration for Magic Flute.

## Maria (Classic Line)

Maria remains one of the most important designs in the Classic Rose group, and one of the most popular dinnerware patterns in the world. It has captured the balance of classical and romantic elements of style and still kept a place on the everyday table, not reserving its use for festive occasions. With many different pieces, not all in production at one time, Maria is the largest of Rosenthal's lines. Lead glass bowls and candlesticks with a delicate flower-like relief outline complement the line. Originally conceived by the founder of the firm and named for his wife, Maria was and continues to be made in solid white. Several decorations have since added interest to the polygonal shapes.

The line has been constantly refreshed with additional pieces over the years. Some of these include: Pickle Dish, Crescent Salad Plate, Butter Dish, Bread Baker, Egg Cup, Bread Board, Pin Bowl, Napkin Ring, four Vases, Oil and Vinegar Cruets, Warmer, Candlestick, Knife Rest.

### Maria Decorations

Gold Line, Necklace, Charme, Rose Border, Blue Garland, Blackberry, Rustica, Almond Blossom, Summer Flowers, Paradise, Petersburg, Poesie, Animal Life.

Selection of classic Maria line in White.

Maria candlestick.

### Suggested Pricing for Maria

Poesie and Animal Life should be considered at double the following prices .

Dinner Plate: $32-$60
Salad Plate: $17-$40
Bread & Butter Plate: $12-$30
Coffee Cup: $21-$60
Saucer: $13-$20
Tea Cup: $21-$60
Saucer: $13-$20
Rim Soup: $25-$65
Fruit Dish: $21-$55
Creamsoup Cup: $30-$75
Creamsoup Saucer: $20-$40
Covered Vegetable: $220-$450
Sauceboat: $85-$175
Open Vegetable, 27 oz.: $60-$80
Open Vegetable, 48 oz.: $80-$125
Cake Plate: $55-$100
Sandwich Tray: $80-$125
Platter, 13": $90-$120
Platter, 15": $146-$185
Salt Shaker: $18-$30
Pepper Shaker: $18-$30
Coffee Pot: $130-$200
Tea Pot: $130-$200
Sugar Bowl: $48-$75
Creamer: $32-$55

"Rustica" decoration on Maria.

# Monbijou (Classic Line)

Given that Monbijou is French for "My Jewel," this line reflects the late Rococo period with charm and grace. No other shape reflects the traditional beauty of porcelain more than this Monbijou. The delicate ornamental self-detailed scrollwork in a tiny leaf and tendril treatment is carefully executed to lend a festive quality to this classically elegant shape. The delicate decorations used on it are enhanced by the dainty shapes of the line. A glass line especially designed to accompany Monbijou sets the table in a wonderful way. Additional pieces, made in some decorations, were: Pickle Dish, Egg Cup with Saucer, Fruit Saucer, Several Vases and a Candlestick.

Selection of Monbijou dinnerware in White.

**Monbijou Decorations:**

Belvedere, Gold Border, Rambouillet, Green Tendril, Elegance, Flower Carpet, Josephine, Catherine, Iris, Louisa Gold

**Suggested Pricing for Monbijou**

Lower pricing here is for the white, undecorated line. "Rambouillet," "Josephine," and "Elegance" may be considered at the high end of the range.

Dinner Plate: $32-$75
Salad Plate: $18-$35
B & B Plate: $13-$25
Coffee Cup: $20-$55
Saucer: $12-$30
Rim Soup: $27-$70
Fruit Dish: $20-$45
Creamsoup Cup: $36-$125
Creamsoup Saucer: $16-$45
Covered Vegetable: $200-$500
Sauceboat: $70-$190
Open Vegetable, 50 oz.: $65-$150

Open Vegetable, 76 oz.: $85-$180
Platter, 13": $75-$150
Platter, 15": $100-$250
Salt Shaker: $19-$50
Pepper Shaker: $19-$50
Coffee Pot: $100-$300
Tea Pot: $100-$300
Sugar: $49-$125
Creamer $32-$100
Vase, 4 1/2": $42-$52
Candlestick: $54-$68

Monbijou
"Belvedere"

Monbijou
"Rambouillet"

## *Mythos (Studio Line)*
### Designed by Paul Wunderlich

Classical and elegant, Mythos (#19300) presented its theme in several colors, all gilded, all in a large tableware offering. Wunderlich decorated several patterns for Mythos, all of which center on a feather relief shown in the original white design. In "Aurata," he chose a pale green, highlighted with gold to compliment the white and gold feather. "Argenta" follows the same treatment, using a pastel blue. Deep colors with a suggestion of a counter wave set "Icaria" apart and "Thalia," in slightly different shades remains colorful. All of the decorations show the gold highlighted leaf in white, Wunderlich's signature for the line. The plates are oval in shape, the handles and finials wing detailed. Mythos is a poetic departure from the form and function of much of Rosenthal's work, but the sum of the pieces provide an important addition to the dinnerware lines.

Paul Wunderlich's shapes seemed well suited to the decoration which Gianni Versace used on them. "Barocco," an elaborate pattern of black, ochre, and umber with a good measure of gold, has been likened to a modern interpretation of mosaics of Ancient Greece. The central medallion shows a deity around which scrollwork and acanthus leaves are draped. "Medusa," very similar in treatment, shows a broader use of color, emphasizing the Gorgon's Head. "Treasures of the Sea" suggests Mediterranean waters, the scent of sea breezes, blue skies. Sea creatures, mythic and actual, appear on different items as if cast up by the tides. The decoration is very Italian, very mysterious, very wonderful.

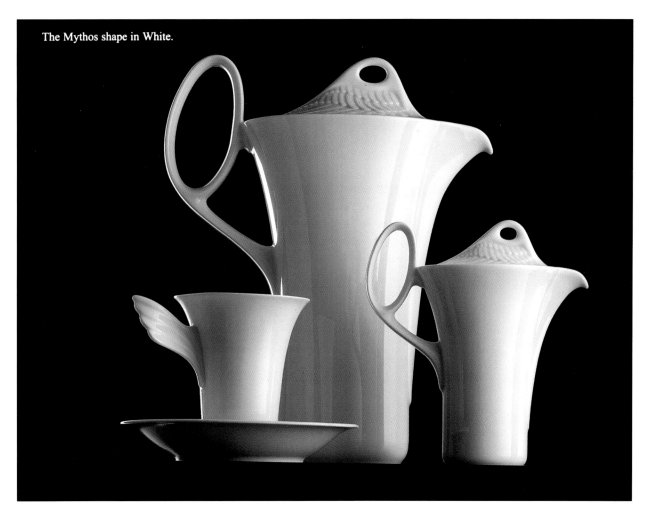

The Mythos shape in White.

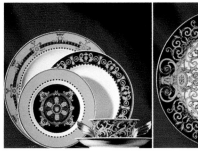

Versaces's "Barocco" decoration on Mythos.

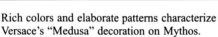

Rich colors and elaborate patterns characterize Versace's "Medusa" decoration on Mythos.

**Suggested Pricing for Mythos**

Service Plate: $195-$200
Dinner Plate: $85-$100
Salad Plate: $60-$75
B & B Plate: $55-$65
Cup, low: $145-$155
Saucer: $50-$55
Cup, high: $145-$165
Saucer $50-$55

A.D. Cup: $110-$125
A.D. Saucer: $40-$50
Rim Soup: $75-$85
Creamsoup Cup: $220-$235
Creamsoup Saucer: $55-$60
Fruit: $80-$90
Tureen: $850-$1,000
Covered Vegetable: $695-$750
Sauceboat: $350-$385
Salad Bowl, 40 oz.: $195-$225

Salad Bowl, 55 oz.: $250-$275
Salad Bowl, 112 oz.: $295-$325
Platter, 13 1/2": $175-$195
Platter, 15 3/4": $225-$250
Coffee Pot: $495-$550
Tea Pot: $495-$550
Covered Sugar: $195-$225
Creamer: $275-$295

"Treasures of the Sea," another Versace decoration on Mythos, reflects the designer's Italian heritage.

## Palladiana, Heliada, Il Sole di Capri (Classic Line)
**Designed by Piero Fornasetti**

Palladiana, a full sized dinnerware line by Piero Fornasetti, draws upon classic themes and illusion to achieve a fantasy dinnerware line suggesting imaginary architectural treatments. Translated into porcelain, this trompe-l'oeil decoration combines a two-dimensional decoration with a three-dimensional shape, achieving a result beyond that of many artists. The line is fresh, interesting, and surprising. On some of the same shapes, Rosenthal translated Fornasetti's passion for the sun into their "Il Sole di Capri," a line of gift articles. Unusual and delightful, they show Rosenthal's ability to adapt the newness of the '90s into its Classic Line. With a carefree mood, their blue background and golden suns conjure the waters and beaches of the Mediterranean.

Heliada, another dinnerware line, understates formality and carries the sun and it's energy into an expression of warmth and joy. Fornasetti's talents created more than five hundred versions of the same woman's face for his "Temi e Variazioni." A teapot was made in limited editions as were wall plates (sometimes called Julia plates), all inspired by a face he had seen by chance in a nineteenth century magazine. This line addresses the timeliness of the Classic line, bringing it up to tomorrow.

Selection of the architecturally inspired Palladinia line, designed by Piero Fornasetti.

"Il Sole di Capri," a line of colorful, original gift items.

Teapots from Fornasetti's "Temi e Variazioni" series, all featuring the same woman's face.

### Suggested Pricing for Palladiana and Heliada

Palladiana items are represented by the high end, Heliada items by the lower figures.

Service Plate: $195-$225
Dinner Plate: $80-$100
Salad/Dessert Plate: $60-$65
B & B Plate: $50-$55
Cup, high: $105-$115
Saucer: $55-$60
Cup, low: $105-$120
Saucer: $55-$60
A.D. Cup: $75-$100
A.D. Saucer: $50-$55
Rim Soup: $75-$85
Creamsoup Cup, 7 oz.: $115-$125
Creamsoup Saucer: $60-$70
Creamsoup, 10 1/2 oz.: $135-$150
Creamsoup Saucer: $90-$95
Fruit: $95-$110

Tureen: $550-$650
Covered Vegetable: $450-$550
Sauceboat: $325-$350
Salad Bowl, 50 oz.: $275-$300
Stand for Platter: $215-$235
Platter, 13": $275-$300
Platter, 15": $325-$350
Coffee Pot: $375-$400
Tea Pot: $375-$400
Warmer: $165-$185
Covered Sugar: $190-$200
Creamer: $140-$150
Covered Butter Dish: $275-$325
Egg Cup: $55-$75
Shakers, pair: $135-$150

**Palladiana Accessory Items**

Vase, 4": $49-$65
Vase, 5 1/2": $98-$135
Vase, 7 1/2": $125-$150
Vase, oval 8": $165-$200
Vase, 9": $159-$200
Tray, 5": $98-$125
Tray, square, 8 1/2": $149-$175
Box, wide, 3": $59-$75
Box, tall, 4 1/4": $175-$200
Tumbler: $59-$85
Mug: $69-$100
Candlestick: $69-$100
Coaster, 4": $29-$40

## Polygon (Studio Line)
**Designed by Tapio Wirkkala**

As originally conceived, Polygon White (#1600) is angular in relief, allowing light and shadow to reflect in an interesting manner. Architectural design characteristics, primary in Wirkkala's compositions, are, not surprisingly, expressed in this work. The design, highly functional and practical, seems carefully executed to the exceptional degree which Wirkkala has always extended in his work.

The Rosenthal Studio decorations on Polygon included "Korfu," with a thin gold line on the rim of some items, vertical gold lines following the relief of the shape on others, highlighting the shape in an unusual direction. "Korinth" details a horizontal linear treatment with a spaced geometrical symbol, all in cobalt, again producing a strong contrast. "Sunion" has apple green bands completely circling the shapes, a return once more to the contrast of shape and design. J. Klocker's "Thebes" decoration uses evenly spaced horizontal cobalt lines. "Pates," an altogether different design, by French artist Alain Le Foll, incorporates a large and colorful floral band to encircle the borders of plates and positions it interestingly on larger pieces as though it had grown from the bottom

to a garden of pastel flowers. Bjorn Wiinblad's fanciful and imaginative embellishing "Serenade" is an elaborate tracery of flowers, trees and figures, scenic in effect, filling the shape with a bounty of blue detail and with the imaginative treatment which he brings to all his work. "Rhodos," a romantic floral decoration which Rut Bryk applied to Polygon, is a restrained floral application of forget-me-not forms in a colorful but delicate style which allowed trails of flower and vines to extend downward, taking advantage of Polygon's vertical relief. Just as interesting is her "Winter Journey," upon which she details stylized trees with bare branches, doorways and windows reflecting subdued colors against the wintry white landscape of the shape. "Milos" by Kathy Still shows wild grasses, adding movement to the geometric shape. Eduardo Paolozzi treats the Polygon shape with a graphic design he named "Palladio" after the Renaissance architect Andrea Palladio. Obviously a graphic designer, Paolozzi uses design elements of technical drawings, resulting in a two-dimensional architectural arabesque with different motifs on each part of the service. "Palladio" combines shape and decoration in one of the most interesting Polygon examples. Vases and candleholders complement the service. Barbara Brenner's colorful abstract decorations relieve the architectural shapes, while "Korfu," a studio treatment,

Selection of Polygon dinnerware in White.

50

Rut Bryk's "Winter Journey" decoration on Polygon.

"Korfu" decoration on Polygon.

double lines them, accenting the shape with simple elegance. "Liniature" by the designer Yang, follows the shape of the items with a faceted linear decoration alternating with geometrical symbols. The result is restrained, allowing the shape to direct the decoration. Late, but important decorations on the Polygon shape have been done by Gianni Versace. Dramatic in scale, rich in color, they follow the ornate designs we have come to associate with Versace's work. "The Voyage of Marco Polo," in brilliant color, allows each item to tell its own story of the Far East, fabled with the elegance and courtly style unique to it. We find colorful peacocks in glorious color and camel riders adorning the plates. "The Sun God," equally detailed, allows us to see portions of the pattern in different items, but the central medallion, the sun mask of Louis XIV, translates to a bold fruit pattern on some items, a trace of a courier on others. All are unified by festoons, putti here, griffins and an Inca king there.

Wonderful tall glass stemware, also designed by Versace, is gold bordered in a greek-key type design but the eye is drawn at once to the frosted sun god, a signature for diners.

Old, but new in many ways, Polygon has proved its place in Rosenthal's most admired shapes.

Helmut Adler designed a stainless steel group to coordinate with Polygon and named it Austria. Wirkkala himself designed Variation, a cut-footed crystal group as a companion line.

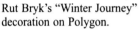

**Above:**
Blue and white Polygon "Serenade."

**Left:**
Graphic designer Eduardo Paolozzi designed "Palladio" for the Polygon shape.

## Suggested Pricing for Polygon

Versace decorations are at the high end of the scale, less detailed patterns at the lower end.

Service Plate: $195-$225
Dinner Plate: $80-$100
Salad/Dessert Plate: $60-$65
B & B Plate: $50-$55
Cup, high: $105-$115
Saucer: $55-$60
Cup, low: $105-$120
Saucer: $55-$60
A.D. Cup: $75-$100
A.D. Saucer: $50-$55
Rim Soup: $75-$85
Creamsoup Cup, 7 oz.: $115-$125
Creamsoup Saucer: $60-$70
Creamsoup, 10 1/2 oz.: $135-$150
Creamsoup Saucer: $90-$95
Fruit: $95-$110
Tureen: $550-$650
Covered Vegetable: $450-$550
Sauceboat: $325-$350

Salad Bowl, 50 oz.: $275-$300
Stand for Platter: $215-$235
Platter, 13": $275-$300
Platter, 15": $325-$350
Coffee Pot: $375-$400
Tea Pot: $375-$400
Warmer: $165-$185
Covered Sugar: $190-$200
Creamer: $140-$150
Covered Butter Dish: $275-$325
Egg Cup: $55-$75
Shakers, pair: $135-$150

**Left:**
Polygon's geometrically-oriented "Liniature" decoration.

**Far left:**
Polygon Coffee Cup in "Sunion."

Gianni Versace designed this exotic "Voyage of Marco Polo" decoration for the Polygon shape.

Versace's equally sumptuous decoration for Polygon, "The Sun God."

## Romance (Classic Line)

This classic shape, created in 1959 by Bjorn Wiinblad and also known as Romanze, found a favored position with those who prefer more traditional styles. Self-patterned, a net relief of small oval forms, dots, and stripes create a lace-like surface. Applied graceful handles, beautifully arched, add detail to the shape as do the domed and mushroom shaped covers. The pattern rays out from the center of the plate to the enlarged detail at the rim, beautifully revealing the self detail. Few decorations were used on this shape and those add only light detail to this '50s line which has captures old world romanticism. Romance glass stemware and tumblers as well as coordinating cutlery were especially designed to accompany the line.

### Romance Decorations

Romanze Secunda Gold, Romanze in B-Major, Romance in Blue, Medley, Romance, White, Campana, Garland, Quatre Coleurs, Orchid, Primavera.

### Suggested Pricing for Romance

The low end of these prices represents white only. Other decorations should be considered higher, depending upon complexity of design. "Campagna" is valued at double these prices.

Dinner Plate: $37-$75
Salad Plate: $18-$40
B & B Plate: $10-$25
Coffee Cup: $20-$40
Saucer: $13-$20
Tea Cup: $20-$40
Saucer: $13-$20
Coupe Soup: $28-$50
Fruit Bowl: $18-$45
Creamsoup Cup: $36-$55
Creamsoup Saucer: $24-$38
Soup Tureen: $275-$400
Covered Vegetable: $195-$350
Sauceboat: $80-$135
Open Vegetable, 8": $110-$200
Open Vegetable, 8 1/2": $130-$175
Platter, 13": $110-$145
Platter, 15": $140-$180
Coffee Pot: $135-$225
Tea Pot: $135-$200
Sugar: $50-$80
Creamer: $40-$70

"Romance in Blue"

Romance "Quatre Couleurs"

Romance "Orchid"

**Next page:** "Romanze in B-Major"

## Sanssouci (Classic Line)

The pleasure palace of Frederick the Great inspired the shape and detail of this ageless porcelain line. Rosenthal presented it in both white and ivory glazes and used it as a background for some of its most ornate decorations. Said to faithfully reproduce the trailing vines found in the palace park as well as the reflected detail in the ceilings of the palace, Sanssouci brought majesty to the table. Though Sanssouci was a large dinnerware line, it was also suggested as an After Dinner group which would include a Coffee Pot, Cream and Sugar, and Cups and Saucers. Additional items included: Pickle Dish, Warmer, Egg Cup with Saucer, Decorative Box, Fruit Saucer, Candlestick, Vases, Table Bell.

### Sanssouci White Decorations

Gold Band, Rose, Fruits, Jessica, Michelle, Pastel Flowers, Platinum Band, Royale, Sanssouci Rose (without Gold).

### Sanssouci Ivory Decorations

Barbara, Diplomat, Moss Rose, Ramona, Arcadia, Jennifer.

### Suggested Pricing for Sanssouci

Prices given are for White and Ivory. Gold banded decorations are about 25 percent higher, floral decorations 50 percent higher.

Dinner Plate, 10 1/4": $35-$100
Salad Plate, 7 1/2": $20-$55
B & B Plate, 5 3/4": $15-$35
Cup, 7 3/4 oz.: $20-$60
Saucer: $13-$35
Cup, 7 oz.: $20-$55
Saucer: $13-$35
A.D. Cup, 3 oz.: $15-$50
A.D. Saucer: $12-$35
Rim Soup, 8 1/4": $30-$80
Fruit, 5 3/4": $20-$45
Creamsoup Cup, 10 1/2 oz.: $35-$100
Creamsoup Saucer: $25-$65
Tureen, 132 oz.: $315-$750
Covered Vegetable, 50 oz.: $200-$550
Sauceboat, 22 oz.: $90-$325
Open Vegetable, 48 oz.: $75-$200
Open Vegetable, 27 oz.: $60-$175
Cake Plate, handled: $65-$200
Oval Platter, 15": $150-$300
Oval Platter, 13": $75-$200
Coffeepot, 37 oz.: $100-$300
Tea Pot, 42 oz.: $125-$300
Sugar Bowl, 8 3/4 oz.: $40-$150
A.D. Sugar Bowl: $30-$125
Creamer, 6 1/2 oz.: $30-$110
A. D. Creamer: $25-$100
Covered Butter Dish: $90-$200
Tort Tray: $100-$200
Fruit/Bread Basket: $100-$275

Selection of Sanssouci
dinnerware in White.

Sanssouci White coffee service.

## Scenario (Studio Line)
**Designed by Barbara Brenner**

Barbara Brenner brings relaxation to a festive dinner with her Scenario line (#22800). Ms. Brenner extends her design philosophy as she makes room for this colorful, unconventional style on a contemporary table.

Drawing upon architecture for its fundamental shape, the colorfully decorated line is casual, inviting diners to lose themselves in the interplay of line and color. The pattern "Metropol" combines all of these signature influences, with strikingly colored borders playing beside black and white dotted accents. The dinnerware is informal, perfectly expressed, but the Grill Table which Brenner designed as a backdrop for the line is a modern miracle. Just right for supper outside, it can be moved to a family room where it is equally appropriate. The center of the table can be fitted with a round ceramic cover, a grill, or an oversized frying pan. The table is 29" high and 48" wide. It has a reinforced concrete ring and holds a grill grate, a charcoal burner, and an ash bucket, as well as an insert ring which could cover the inner cooking unit. Patterns included Blue or Brown as well as the Scenario pattern. The table top is composed of six segments and a cover plate and includes a grill with grate, charcoal burner, and a draft regulator. Brenner also designed a fantasy fruit/floral decoration named "Natura" which combined a lively border on place setting pieces with complete coverage on larger serving items. It is less colorful, but just as unconventional as "Metropol." Both are fanciful, versatile, delightful to use in a large collection of pots, pans, tureens—all designed for an informal table. A full line of cutlery duplicates the Metropol decoration and adds to the interest of the group.

**Suggested Pricing for Scenario**

Service Plate: $70-$150
Dinner Plate: $30-$60
Salad Plate: $28-$45
Fruit: $37-$50
Cup and Saucer, high: $45-$50
A.D. Cup & Saucer: $55-$60
Tureen: $350-$400
Covered Vegetable Dish: $225-$250
Open Vegetable Bowl, 3 sizes: $100-$300
Sauceboat & Stand: $85-$100
Cheese Platter: $50-$65
Shakers: $40-$50
Coffee Pot: $150-$200
Sugar: $70-$80
Creamer: $50-$60
Covered Butter: $115-$130
Beer Stein (Mug), small: $75-$90
Beer Stein, large: $85-$100
Covered Box: $75-$100
Ashtray: $40-$50
Cruets: $125-$150
Grill Table: NPD

The uniquely designed Scenario Grill Table, designed by Barbara Brenner.

**Above and right:** Selection of
Scenario dinnerware in "Metropol."

Scenario "Natura" decoration.

## Spirit (Studio Line)
### Designed by Dorothy Hafner

Hafner's futuristic Spirit shape (#24520) and the "Signa" design with which she decorated it, combines bulges and roundings, contoured in waves with finials which stretch to another dimension. Colorful, it suggests cosmic yearnings, reaching out to the interests in other planets, other worlds. It is the perfect background for the delightful lighthearted decorations done on it by Yang and Brigitte Doege. Yang's decoration "Freestyle" sets his abstract, brightly colored patterns against Hafner's shapes, changing the feel of the line completely and adding a liveliness to the shape. Brigitte Doege's "Wonderland," with more serene colors and dynamic movement, contrast the gentle flow of the shape. Spirit and its decorations are of late production, but very important contributions to ceramic art in dinnerware.

### Suggested Pricing for Spirit

Dinner Plate, 10 1/2": $48-$100
Salad Plate, 8 1/2": $32-$50
B & B Plate, 7": $30-$60
Cup & Saucer, high: $57-$75
A.D. Cup & Saucer: $55-$75
Creamsoup: $50-$65
Fruit: $30-$50
Vegetable bowl, small: $85-$100
Vegetable bowl, medium: $110-$200
Vegetable bowl, large: $145-$250
Soup Tureen: $360-$400
Sauceboat, 2 pieces: $150-$200
Platter, 10 1/4": $70-$125
Platter, 13 1/4": $125-$150
Platter, 15": $200-$250
Coffee Pot: $170-$200
Tea Pot: $170-$200
Sugar: $65-$80
Creamer: $50-$60
Cake Plate, 12 1/2": $100-$150

Selection of Spirit dinnerware in the "Signa" decoration, designed by Dorothy Hafner.

Yang's "Freestyle" decoration on Spirit.

Brigitte Doege's "Wonderland" decoration on Spirit.

# Suomi (Studio Line)
## Designed by Timo Sarpaneva

Sarpaneva is said to have found the source for his Suomi shape (#17000) in the movement of a river, as it rounds and smoothes a stone. Organic in shape, it challenges its contours, reaching for harmony between circles and squares. It has been awarded the highest honor of the porcelain world, The Faenza Gold Medal. Perhaps no other line has captured the imagination of so many other artists, for many of them decorated the shape, adding to many concepts. Some developed variations for dinnerware lines, but others, believing the shape to be a perfect canvas, used it to express their art for smaller lines, for accessory items as well. Easily a favorite of modernists, it is a luminary line in the work which Rosenthal offered in its Studio Line.

Sarpaneva designed Suomi in white and it was difficult to improve upon that pure statement. He did, however, add a "Black and White," using some items in solid white, others in solid black, achieving an effect only slightly less sophisticated than the classic white. "Suomi Anthracite," a Rosenthal Studio decoration, added a black linear treatment, often a double line at rims and brims. Decorating Suomi with an oriental motif, the studio named another decoration "Shou," a free translation of the oriental long life symbol. "Suomi Lanka," another Studio treatment, drew a fine silver line at the brim and inner rim. "White Gold" differed in that it also incorporated larger amounts of the metal contrast, coloring covers and wider borders. "Polished Gold" made the same statement, an elegant one, using the richness of gold in lavish amounts. Yatta Svennevig decorated "Suomi Linja" with varying width vertical white gold bands. Geometrically treated, it allows one to see the many types of decorations which could be used on the shape. Alain Le Foll decorated Suomi with "Roseau," a delicately shaded naturalistic decoration. "Suomi Sea Rose," by Gisela Muller-Behrendt, is a delicate but generously scaled print, with subtle color nuances reminiscent of the graphic works of Asian artists. "Suomi White Orchid," by Yang, treats the shape with a delicate floral tracery. Yang brought Suomi into tomorrow with his "Suomi Aristo," treating the borders with a pastel band with metal-like accents. In "Collage," Brigitte Doege colored the plate rims in a brilliant blue, using a riot of colors on cups and serving pieces. She used an inner rim band of the same colors in her "Suomi Bandella." "Suomi Gala," a Studio decoration, added a wide band of lustrous polished platinum, pointing to the diverse treatments which could be used on this shape, each achieving a different interpretation.

A unique treatment done on the Suomi shape was that done by Lord Queensberry and named "Queensberry Marble." Abstract clouds, converging waters, veined suggestions of wood and marble unite to effect the phenomenon of microscopically small crystalline forms. It is a work of nature's art brought to the pieces, never exactly the same, always decorated with the structural art of the elements.

"Queensberry Marble" cannot be produced by standard methods and a great deal of handwork selectively designed each piece in an exclusive way. It has been said that it is the creativity of chance, done in an exacting way so as to preserve the two-colored effect, allowing for flowing lines and contours. Much of it is rejected in the final process of production but what remains is of very individual quality achieved by skilled craftsmen. You will find it in shades of grey, rose, and brown.

Each piece of Suomi expresses roundness of structure, while still achieving compact shape, secure to the hand. The hoop band on the pot, sauceboat, and covered vegetable dish accents the form.

The beauty of the porcelain was made even more beautiful by the addition of stainless steel cutlery which incorporated oval shaping on its matte handles. The bowls of the spoons reflect the rounded Suomi shape.

Selection of Suomi dinnerware in White.

"Collage" decoration on Suomi, by Brigitte Doege.

Suomi "Shou," meaning "Long Life."

"Roseau" on Suomi, designed by Alain Le Foll.

## Suggested Pricing for Suomi

Dinner Plate: $50-$65
Salad/Dessert Plate: $20-$30
B & B Plate: $14-$40
Cup: $27-$35
Saucer: $15-$20
A.D. Cup: $24-$40
A.D. Saucer: $12-$15
Service Plate, 11": $85-$150
Fruit: $35-$50
Rim Soup: $32-$50
Creamsoup Cup: $55-$75
Creamsoup Saucer: $20-$25
Open Vegetable, 64 oz.: $90-$200
Open Vegetable, 87 oz.: $110-$300
Open Vegetable, 160 oz.: $195-$400
Covered Vegetable: $325-$500
Sauceboat & Stand: $225-$300
Platter, 13": $110-$200
Platter, 15": $150-$200
Coffee Pot: $150-$200
Tea Pot: $150-$250
Sugar: $75-$150
Creamer: $75-$150
Shakers, pair: $40-$60

**Above:**
Yatta Svennevig's "Linja" on Suomi.

**Left:**
Yang's "Aristo" decoration on Suomi.

**Opposite:**
Suomi in the Black and White variation.

"Queensberry Marble," designed by Lord Queensberry, was one of the most distinctive treatments on the Suomi shape. These photos show the subtle lines and color variations of this naturalistic decoration.

## Untitled and Sienna (Studio Line)

Untitled, another Wiinblad shape, was originally applied to a ceramic table pattern but it quickly found a place with two collections of glass goblets, decorative pewter plates, and stainless steel cutlery with ceramic handles. One unusual and distinctive decoration is "Till Eulenspiegel," in which Wiinblad illustrated more than forty scenes from Till's adventures on the Untitled shape. The designs, different on each piece, are hand painted in a delightful folksy style unlike any other designs mentioned here. Cartoon-like, it is easily identified once seen. A similar shape, Sienna, was used for a very large collection, often seen with Untitled. Wiinblad decorated it as a hand painted full ceramic table service including a coffee service as well as a sturdy glass collection. A Grill Set, with a large number of special items ranging from fondue sets and beer mugs to a special brandy set and even a luxury grill table, add to Sienna's uses. All of these are compatible with Untitled.

NPD on this recent, but interesting, large group.

Wiinblad's Untitled shape, shown here with his "Till Eulenspiegel" decoration.

Pewter plates in the Untitled shape.

The Sienna shape is similar to Untitled; they are often seen together.

65

## Variation (Studio Line)
**Designed by Tapio Wirkkala**

Variation (#40 5000) combines white porcelain with a black porcelain, not only glazed black but black in composition, rare and expensive to produce. Architecturally shaped, Variation contrasts a smooth surface with one on which there is relief. The "White with Black" variation coupled white pieces with black knobs. A modification of that decoration was named "Shadow Play;" it was done by the Studio and incorporated the use of black with more restraint. "Cobalt" uses a dark cobalt blue to rim the plates and accent knobs, affording a horizontal use of color against a vertical shape detail. In "Polar Flower," a decoration by Rut Bryk, we find fine grass buds, suggestive of those found on the tundras of Finland. The decoration lies within the grooves of the relief, adding delicacy to the colored grasses. A fragile and lacy decoration, it follows the vertical lines, extending itself in different heights, playing easily on the shape it decorates. Ivan Rabuzin's "Ljubica" on the Variation shape was the painter's vision of a flowering meadow near his Croatian home. Adding contrast to the structured surface of the shape, it achieved a rhythmic, informal quality, never at odds with the shape.

Glassware, cutlery, and accessory items, all designed by Wirkkala, added to the complete tableware group.

### Suggested Pricing for Variation

Dinner Plate: $30-$40
Salad Plate: $20-$22
B & B Plate: $13-$17
Cup and Saucer: $40-$50
Vegetable Bowl: $75-$95
Platter: $125-$150
Vase, 4": $50-$60

**Above:**
The Variation shape.

**Left:**
Variation "Polar Flower," by Rut Bryk.

Variation "Cobalt"

66

## *Drop Tea Service*
**Designed by Luigi Colani**

The Drop Tea Service is a result of thorough functional studies done by the designer. One's hand goes right to the teapot's center of gravity and pouring from the vessel is done without effort. The cups have small feet so that any liquid spilled does not collect around the bottom of the cup. The cup handles are bigger for easier holding. Organic in shape, the concave body has a spout extending from the shape itself, while the kidney shaped body has an integral grip. The cover is flat and round, to be inserted into the body. The Tea Pot is accompanied by a Creamer, a Sugar, a Cup and Saucer as well as a Dessert Plate. The Drop service is a delight to Modernists, who view it as modern elegance.

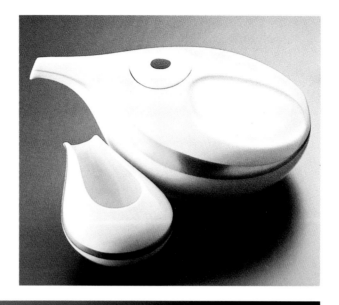

The Drop Tea Service, shown in both White and White with Gold.

## Empire New

Empire New was a tea service dating from 1910. Its green underglaze is decorated with a blue dice border treatment, often duplicated at the top and bottom of the piece. The Teapot is 4 5/8" high. Flat handles accent the geometric banded decoration. Sets may be valued from $125-$185.

## Gropius Tea Service
### Designed by Walter Gropius

The Gropius Tea Service (Taci), designed by the artist whose name is synonymous with the Bauhaus, has long been recognized as a benchmark in table service design. Louis McMillen contributed to the perfection which its admirers claim for it. Many feel that this design has never been surpassed in excellence of form or decoration. It has been said that Gropius was guided by the idea of an inversion of teapot and bowl in mirror symmetry, combining a gloss glaze with a bisque finish. He designed this streamlined tea service in white or black, depending upon glazed and matte finishes within the same item for interest. The small line included the Teapot, with a glazed insert for tea leaves, a Covered Sugar, Creamer, Teacup and Saucer, and a 7 1/2" Dessert Plate. While it is difficult to conceive of any improvement on this masterpiece in porcelain, many others have decorated it in ways that are also important. The following are some of those decorations: "Gropius Twenty-Five," by Yang; "Fatamorgana," by Rainer Fetting; "Architee," by M. Morandini; "Green Tree," by Arnulf Rainer; "Poisonous Snake," by Elvira Bach; "Faces," by Sandro Chia; "Avalon," by O.H. Hajek; "Fox Rest," by C. Attersee; "Derevolution," by Sergei Bugaev; "Hearts," by P. Giovanopoul; "Russian Teapot," by I. Kopystiansky; "Mekka-No," by E. Paolozzi; "Vocals," by J. Immendorf; "Bauhaus Hommage," by Herbert Bayer; and "Stripes," which is not documented.

Suggested values on these decorations, all works of art on a fine art shape, cannot be priced here. The original Taci in a White twenty-three piece Tea Set may be valued at $1000, in Black at $1500.

The Empire New tea service.

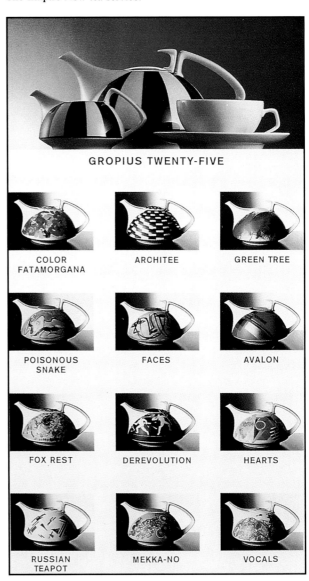

Selection of decorations on the Gropius Tea Service.

The Gropius Tea
Service, shown in
White and Black.

# Thomas Stoneware

## Scandic

This Thomas line, pleasing to the eye in white, red, orange, or green, as well as in several linear decorations, is youthful and dynamic, suiting the needs of the cook and maintaining the needs of the hostess. The large item listing extends itself to porcelain pots that were specially designed to keep foods warm, while other flame proof pots and casseroles were specially designed to be used in frying and roasting with electricity, gas, or microwave. Items were designed for dual usage, adding to their informal quality.

**Suggested Pricing for Scandic**

White is at the lower end of the price range, "Fjord" at the highest end.

Dinner Plate: $10-$20
Salad Plate: $6-$10
B & B Plate: $3-$7
Cup and Saucer: $15-$25
Vegetable Bowl: $35-$40
Platter: $40-$60

Selection of Scandic tableware and cookware in White.

Scandic "Rubin"

Scandic "Flower"

Scandic "Green"

Scandic "Orange"

71

# Table Fashion

This very contemporary line expresses color in all its variations, in many treatments from loud and garish to quiet and serene. Add a touch of the hostess' sense of style and tables take on newness achieved by personal preferences. "Stripes," in fresh new shades, combine with "Points," in various color combinations, to achieve a table tailored to mix and match design as well as color. The results are endless and additional decorations, some lively and bright, some less complicated, achieve a line that is outstanding in the Thomas group. These decorations include: "Punti," "Africana," "Sun, Moon and Stars," and "Leaves." Coffee Pots, Tureens and Bowls join place settings, adding up to colorful surprises.

**Suggested Pricing for Table Fashion**

NPD

Table Fashion "Points" and "Stripes"
mix and match with flair.

Table Fashion "Sun, Moon and Stars" decoration.

"Africana" decoration on Table Fashion features geometric and giraffe inspired patterns.

Table Fashion "Punti"

Table Fashion "Leaves"

73

## Tournee

With a bit of elegance, modern and unconventional, but with careful attention to detail, Tournee is charming in design, unsurpassed for its extensive decorations styles. The item listing is large, allowing for elegance from breakfast to dinner. More formal than most Thomas lines, Tournee offers choices seldom found in dinnerware of this price range.

**Suggested Pricing for Tournee**

White is at the lower end of the price range, decorated items at the highest end.

Dinner Plate: $10-$50
Salad Plate: $5-$30
B & B Plate: $20-$25
Vegetable Bowl: $20-$135
Platter: $30-$210

Tournee "Fleury"

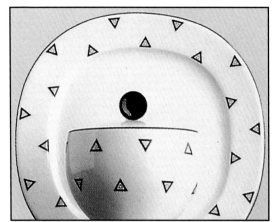

Tournee "Concord"

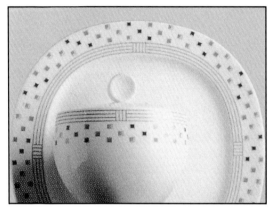

Tournee "Piqué"

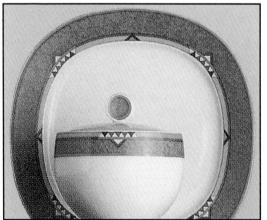

Tournee "Smaragd"

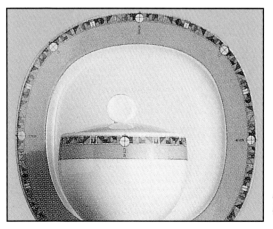

Tournee "Colorit"

**Opposite:**
*Left:* Tournee stoneware in White.
*Right:* Tea served in Tournee "Noir" decoration.

# Trend

The Trend line in Thomas is a large one. China tableware designed for modestly priced daily use, it is accompanied by cork topped canisters for storage, crystal serving bowls, decorative accessories, and cookware designed to be used from oven to table, some even flame proof. Small sizes were especially designed for small microwave use, adding to the large number of pieces. The criteria for practical usage is easily met with stackability, dishwashing safety, large openings for filling pots, pitchers and bowls, and drainage slots in the base rings. Wooden salad bowls and carving boards add extra uses and give Trend the qualities of instant collectibility. Trend decorations are restrained, all typical of the sort of treatment which the Studio Line made popular. White is favored but other decorations shown here illustrate details which seem rooted in Studio Line treatments.

**Suggested Pricing for Trend**

White is at the lower range. "Candy" and "Napoli" are at the highest end.

Dinner Plate: $19-$25
Salad Plate: $10-$15
B & B Plate: $8-$13
Cup & Saucer: $15-$25
Vegetable Bowl: $44-$50
Platter: $65-$75

Trend "Napoli"

Trend "Rio"

Trend "Florida"

**Left:**
Trend "Toscana"

76

# York

Said to have been designed to work in combination with any dining situation, York is contemporary, serving modern needs from teas to buffets, family dinners, or casual brunches. The ovoid line of serving pieces add interest contrasted against the circular plates and round handles. The decorations offer a variety of choices for different lifestyles. York can be dressed up or down with the use of the white pieces, well suited to contrast with the decorated items.

**Suggested Pricing for York**

Dinner Plate: $9-$11
Salad Plate: $5-$7
B & B Plate: $2-$4
Cup and Saucer: $12-$16
Vegetable Bowl: $23-$29
Platter: $35-$43

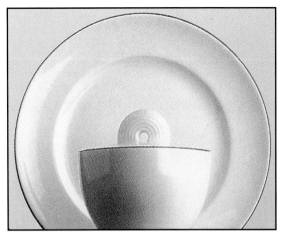

York
"Solo"

York
"Comedy"

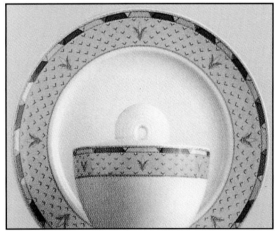

York
"Kronos"

York
"Romba"

"Cubic" decoration on York.

# Cutlery

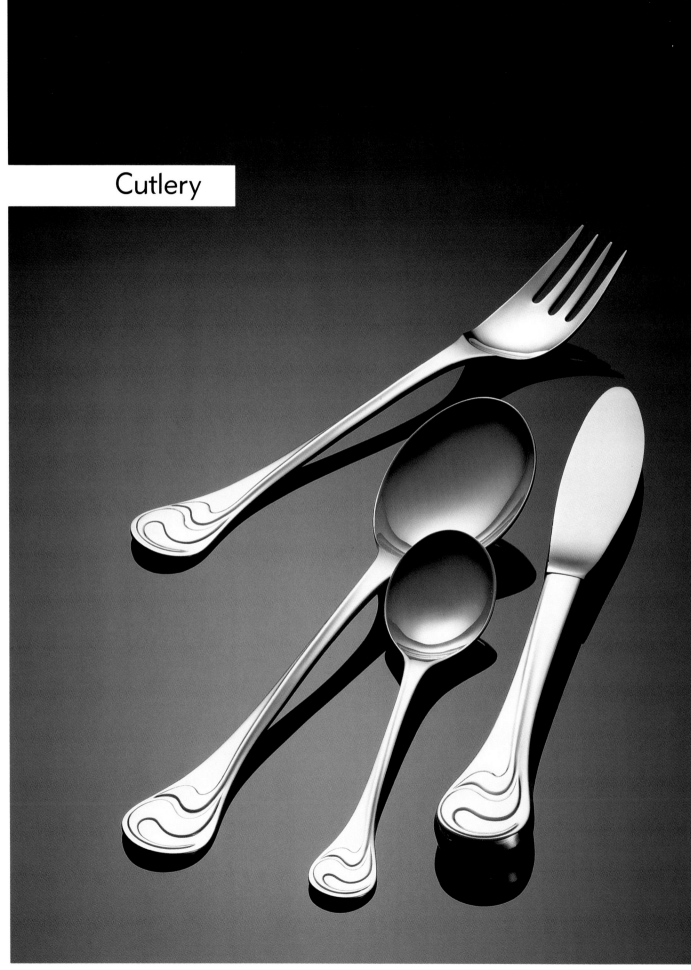

Selection of Asymmetria cutlery.

## *Asymmetria*
### Designed by Bjorn Wiinblad

Asymmetria (#18500/130910) was designed to accompany the dinner service of that same name. The characteristic waves unite the pattern. Perfectly suited to the dinnerware line, it is a contemporary classic with the handle detail adding a romantic quality to any table setting.

### Suggested Pricing for Asymmetria

$30-$100 each item

## *Austria*
### Designed by H. Alder

Austria (#1 2400) speaks to the sort of design which Americans took to their hearts and tables when they first considered Modernism. With flat handles, turned up only for balance, Austria remains up-to-the minute in design.

### Suggested Pricing for Austria

$30-$70 each item.

Selection of
Austria cutlery.

## Berlin
### Designed by H. T. Baumann

Baumann's Berlin (#13000), with long and slender handles, is a classic that draws contrasts between the linear lines of the handles and the curved fork and spoon bowls. Functional to the last item, it could be used anywhere, any time, although it was designed to accompany the Berlin line of dinnerware. Awarded the Dutch Good Design Award, it is among the most outstanding of stainless designs.

### Suggested Pricing for Berlin

$40-$100 each item.

## Brotzeitbesteck
### Designed by Bjorn Wiinblad

This service (#2680) is similar in concept to the Grillbesteck line (see below), though its handles are somewhat more detailed. Made of two colors, the dark blue rosettes on the handle ends are united with a brown, dotted scroll design. At home in informal settings, it included steak sets as well as fondue groups.

### Suggested Pricing for Brotzeitbesteck

$50-$100 each item.

## Cambio
### Designed by Marcello Morandini

Cambio (#18720/130900) is a late design with all the qualities of brushed stainless steel lines which have been so popular over the years. With long, rounded but tapered handles, the line is quickly identified by the prongs of the fork which are interestingly step-shaped.

### Suggested Pricing for Cambio

$30-$100 each item.

## Century
### Designed by Tapio Wirkkala and K. G. Hansen

Century cutlery (#l 8000) presents a pleasing service to use with Wirkkala's Century dinnerware. It combines silver plated bowls, blades, and prongs with porcelain handles capped in silver, highly wear-resistant. Inseparably connected, the silver and metal parts are dishwasher safe.

### Suggested Pricing for Century

$50-$120 each item.

Selection of Berlin cutlery.

Selection of Brotzeitbesteck cutlery.

**Above:**
Fork, knife, and spoon from
the Cambio cutlery line.

**Left:**
Selection of Century cutlery.

Knife, fork, and spoon from the Composition cutlery line.

Knife, spoon, and fork from the Concav cutlery line.

## Composition
### Designed by Tapio Wirkkala

Made of brushed steel, Composition (#13500/130910) was designed for use every day, functionally puristic. All the pieces are forged in one single piece and the knife is based on a parallelogram, transferring force from the hand to the cutting surface of the blade.

**Suggested Pricing for Composition**

$30-$70 each item.

## Concav
### Designed by Claudia Plikat and Carola Zwick

Concav (#18900/13900) is identified by elegantly tapered tips which broaden and merge at the base of the rounded bowls and tines. Sculptured with two such diverse shapes, this polished stainless steel line has an organic quality to it.

**Suggested Pricing for Concav**

$30-$70 each item.

Selection of Dialog cutlery.

## *Dialog*
### Designed by Lino Sabattini

Dialog (#18200/130910) is functional first, with long, clean, and delicate lines. Made of brushed stainless steel, the handles are accented at their ends by a small sphere, carefully applied. While Dialog works well with either formal or ultra formal dinnerware, its shape makes a post modern statement, an unusual one.

### Suggested Pricing for Dialog

$35-$90 each item.

## *Giro*
### Designed by Tile Geismar

Giro (#18800/130900), functionally designed to rest comfortably in the user's hand, is pleasing to the eye as well. Serving items are balanced mid-point to afford easy use. Polished stainless steel, the line makes a contemporary statement.

### Suggested Pricing for Giro

$30-$70 each item.

Selection of Giro cutlery.

# *Grillbesteck*
## Designed by Bjorn Wiinblad

Ceramic-handled cutlery in interesting shapes, combined with the durability of stainless, adds new dimension to Rosenthal's cutlery lines. Done in shades of brown and blue, and with place settings which included serving items as well as sets of fondue forks, this line was a lively informal addition to the stainless lines being done at the same time.

**Suggested Pricing for Grillbesteck**

$50-$100 each item.

Selection of Grillbesteck
cutlery in both colors.

## Kurve
### Designed by Tapio Wirkkala

Kurve (#1 3570) adds to the wonderful world of design done by Wirkkala and offers rounded simple shapes with upturned handles. The pattern has no pretense save the shape of the items; the knife, with its quarter turned handle, is the only exception. Made of brushed stainless steel, Kurve's unadorned elegance finds a place at any table.

### Suggested Pricing for Kurve

$50-$100 each item.

## Lotus
### Designed by Bjorn Wiinblad and K. G. Hansen

Lotus (#1 2660) was meant to add detail to the Lotus dinnerware line. It adds elegance as well and was made in sterling silver as well as a gold plate. The lotus leaves, placed at the ends of the handles, complete the dinner service in a way not possible by using other cutlery.

### Suggested Pricing for Lotus

NPD

**Opposite and right:** Selection of Kurve cutlery.

Selection of Lotus cutlery.

## *Maestro*
### Designed by Harald Lampert

Harald Lampert, named a Young Artist of 1992, designed Maestro (#18730/130900) in a large series of stainless steel cutlery. With a linear pattern on the handles, the line assumes a somewhat formal appearance.

### Suggested Pricing for Maestro

$25-$100 each item.

Selection of Maestro cutlery.

## *Plus*
### Designed by Wolf Karmagel

Plus adds detail to the stainless lines discussed here. The end of the handle is decorated with a simple circle which draws the eye to the length of the piece as it tapers to the broader end.

### Suggested Pricing for Plus

$30-$70 each item.

[Insert Photo 279 here]

Knife, fork, and spoon from the Plus line of cutlery.

## *Romance*
### Designed by Bjorn Wiinblad

Designed by Wiinblad to accompany his Romance dinnerware, this cutlery (#1 2600) was produced in classical style with elements of contemporary detail. It was made from three different materials, sterling silver, alpaca silver plate and stainless steel. It was also available with a gold wash as well as a gold relief ornamentation on the silver handle. Expensive to make, because of the intricate handle detail as well as the smoothing and hand polishing involved, Romance is a valuable and exclusive pattern.

### Suggested Pricing for Romance

NPD

Selection of Romance cutlery with the gold relief ornamentation.

Selection of Romance cutlery.

Selection of Scenario "Metropol" cutlery.

## Scenario "Metropol"
### Designed by Barbara Brenner

Scenario, designed to add complete quality to a table set with dinnerware of the same name, adds interest beyond measure. The handles are specially hardened ceramic in the "Metropol" decoration while the high quality stainless steel balances it in a way that is easy to use, delightful to contemplate.

**Suggested Pricing for Scenario**

NPD

## Sculptura
### Designed by Lino Sabattini

Art on the dining table as expressed by Sculptura (#18100/130910)! The fork and spoon join the bowl and handle with a wave of metal. The knife, equally interesting, has three small parallel openings at the base of the blade. The shape of the fork allows it to be set on the table without touching and soiling the cloth. That balance extends to each item, including the serving pieces. Sculptura brings Op Art to the table.

**Suggested Pricing for Sculptura**

$45-$110 each item.

90

Selection of Sculptura cutlery.

## String
### Designed by Kuno Prey

String (#18700/130900) is a clear cut shape with no pretense of design or decoration except the soft angle which forms the handle. It will appeal to those purists who ask for economy in design.

**Suggested Pricing for String**

$25-$100 each item.

Selection of String cutlery.

## Suomi
### Designed by Timo Sarpaneva

Sarpaneva brings the greatest of Scandinavian design principles to this Suomi (#17000/13910) stainless steel cutlery. The raised center of the handle is made of brushed steel while the rest of the item is polished steel, playing sheen against shine. Simple, but elegant, Suomi is the perfect companion to the dinnerware it was meant to accompany. It fits easily aside most contemporary dinnerware as well.

**Suggested Pricing for Suomi**

$40-$125 each item.

## Taille
### Designed by Tapio Wirkkala

Wirkkala brings his wonderful world of modernism to the Taille cutlery line, with rounded bowls and rounded handles. It has a droplet design which adds contrast while accomplishing balance. Said to be exceptionally soft to the touch, it is satin brushed stainless steel. It blends well with classic dinnerware but its lines soften contemporary tables with equal ease. Taille was made in a 24 Karat gold finish also.

**Suggested Pricing for Taille**

$35-$100 each item.

Selection of Suomi cutlery.

**Above and next page:**
Selection of Taille cutlery.

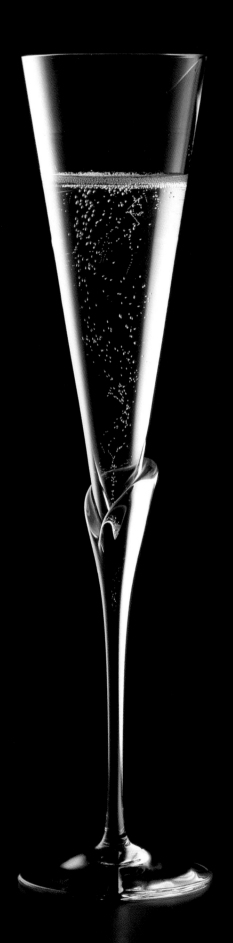

# Glass

Calice glasses.

# Glasses and Stemware

## *Calice and Papyrus*
### Designed by Michael Boehm

Calice and Papyrus differ only in the addition of color to the stem of Papyrus. Michael Boehm has designed stems which seem to spring from an opening bud. Slender and graceful beyond most, these stems speak to elegance and sophistication.

Chalice items include: Beer, Water, White Wine, Red Wine, Port, Liqueur, Champagne Flute, Saucer Champagne, Brandy, Tall Champagne Glass, Riesling Wine, Burgundy, Champagne, Decanter.

Papyrus items include: Beer, Water, White Wine, Red Wine, Port, Liqueur, Champagne Flute, Saucer Champagne, Brandy, Tall Champagne Glass, Burgundy, Decanter.

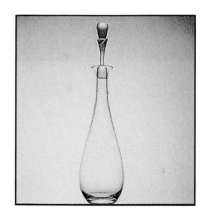

**Suggested Pricing for Calice and Papyrus**

Toasting Champagne: $79
All other stems: $59

Calice glasses and decanter.

## *Caverna*
### Designed by Stuart Garfoot

Designed with a glass lens on the upper part of the stem, this line immediately draws the eye to the surface decoration of the crystal. Said to evoke peace of mind and contemplation, the lens points to the serenity of the shape, drawing only on that feature for detail. The small line included: Water Goblet/Burgundy, White Wine, Red Wine, Champagne Flute, Sherry, Brandy, Gin, and Riesling.

Papyrus

**Suggested Pricing for Caverna**

$40-$60 each stem.

**Right and opposite:**
The Caverna line of glasses.

95

# Chiara

Chiara is an elegantly uncomplicated small glass line which could be at home in any setting. Not intended to accompany a single dinnerware line, these quiet shapes could be used in many ways and with many dinnerware lines. Stem items include: Water/Burgundy, White Wine, Red Wine, Champagne Flute. Tumblers include: Long Drink, Highball, Double Old Fashioned, Old Fashioned, and Shot Glass.

**Suggested Pricing for Chiara**

$15-$19 each stem

Chiara

# Cupola
## Designed by Michael Boehm and Mario Bellini

Cupola, a tall candleholder, may have been inspired by Olympus, but its scale is smaller. Companion Cupola stems were divided, remarkably comfortable to hold. This full lead crystal was elegant enough for formal dining, but durable enough for everyday use. It could be dressed up or down, suiting either a formal or informal occasion. Stems include: Water, 7 3/4"; White Wine, 7 1/2"; Red Wine 7"; Champagne Flute, 8 1/2"; Champagne Sherbet, 6 1/2"; Sherry, 6 1/2"; Liqueur, 6"; Brandy, 6"; and Beer, 7 1/4".

**Suggested Pricing for Cupola**

Stems: $25-$40
Candleholder: $40-$60

Cupola candleholder.

Cupola glasses.

96

## *Estelle*
### Designed by Michael Boehm

A recent addition to Rosenthal's production, Estelle is an elegantly cut pattern making it an ideal companion to use with classic designs. Michael Boehm designed this late glass and it is included here because it gives wonderful dimension to Rosenthal's glass lines. Items include: Goblet, White Wine, Red Wine, Champagne Flute, Sherry, Liqueur, Beer, Brandy, Long Drink, Universal Tumbler/Apertif, Old Fashioned, Double Old Fashioned, Wine and Whiskey Decanters, Water and Ice Jugs, Ice Bucket.

### Suggested Pricing for Estelle

Stems: $29
Pitcher: $175
Decanter, 12 1/2": $149
Whiskey Decanter, 10": $169
Tumblers: $29

Selection of Estelle glasses.

Selection of Estelle glasses and decanter.

## *Fuga*
### Designed by Elsa Fischer-Treyden

Fuga (#10608/110001), mouthblown by Rosenthal's most skilled workers, has a refined but simple shape, allowing it to combine with formal or informal designs, perfect for any occasion. Fuga items include: Water/Beer, Burgundy, White Wine, Red Wine, Liqueur, Champagne Flute, Brandy.

### Suggested Pricing for Fuga

$30-$50 each stem.

## *Julietta*
### Designed by Nanny Still McKinney

Julietta (#20605/110001) is a late line, but its graceful contours, charmingly accented by stem detail, have achieved popularity for the line, establishing it as one collectors admire. Items include: Water Goblet, Burgundy, White Wine, Champagne Flute, Decanter, Pitcher, and Caviar Bowl, as well as 8", 9", and 10" Candleholders.

### Suggested Pricing for Julietta

NPD

**Above and left:** Selection of Fuga glasses.

99

Julietta glasses.

## Lotus Clear
**Designed by Richard Latham**

Chicago designer Richard Latham was inspired by the lotus flower petal as he designed this glass shape (#24000/110001). Pulled from a single piece of glass, the stem and bowl achieve singularity of form, making the design simple but elegant, decidedly useful for many occasions. Lotus Clear was available in: Water Goblet, 7 1/4"; Red Wine, 6 1/2"; White Wine, 6 1/2"; Port, 4 1/2"; Liqueur; Liqueur Saucer; Champagne Flute, 7 3/4"; Champagne Sherbet, 6"; Brandy, 4 1/2"; as well as a Jug and Decanter.

**Suggested Pricing for Lotus Clear**

NPD

## Lotus Blossom
**Designed by Bjorn Wiinblad**

Lotus Blossom (#24000/00730) was designed by Wiinblad to accompany his Lotus shape. The Blossom glassware, in the same items mentioned above, differs in that a lotus blossom pattern is used at the base of the bowl, decorating it with a pattern which harmonized with the porcelain.

**Suggested Pricing for Lotus Blossom**

NPD

**Above:**
Selection of Lotus Clear glasses.

**Left:**
Lotus Blossom

## Maitre
### Designed by Michael Boehm.

With real understanding that the shape of the drinking vessel affects the taste of the drink, Rosenthal sponsored a cooperation of Boehm, a group of wine experts, and fine glass craftsmen. Together they achieved "Maitre" (#10304/110001), said to preserve the specific characteristics of the wine itself while serving it in an elegant manner. The long stems which identify Maitre start with a teardrop below the bowl, narrowing at the base. American glass collectors have admired this shape for many years and it is typically called a "Lady leg stem."

Maitre was divided into two groups, with different bowl shapes. The Bouquet group included: Burgundy, 10 1/4"; White Wine, 8 1/2"; Liqueur, 6 1/2"; French Champagne, 9 1/2"; Champagne Sherbet, 7 1/4"; and a Brandy, 7". The Overt Group included: Red Wine, 10 1/2"; Water Goblet, 9 3/4"; White Wine, 9"; Schnapps, 7 1/4"; and a Champagne Flute, 10".

Maitre

### Suggested Pricing for Maitre

$30-$70 each item for Maitre Bouquet.
$50-$75 each item for Maitre Overt.

## Maria

The counterplay of the round bowl and hexagonal base gives an old world look to this classic glassware. The delicately embossed pattern relates directly to the porcelain which it was designed to accent. Items include: White Wine, Port, Burgundy, Goblet, Wine Tumbler, Long Drink, Multipurpose Glass. Saucer Champagne, Whiskey Tumbler, Dessert Saucer, Champagne Flute, Liqueur Flute, Liqueur Saucer, Brandy, Beer Tulip, Candlestick.

### Suggested Pricing for Maria

$40-$100 each item.

Maria glasses.

**Above:**
Maria glasses.

**Left:**
Maria bowls and candlestick.

104

Monbijou

## Monbijou

The rococo design of this glass shape blends in beautifully with the delicate porcelain it accompanies. Made in either clear or a patterned "Trailing," it takes one's table to another time, another world. Items include: White Wine, Red Wine, Burgundy, Port, Champagne Flute, Saucer Champagne, Brandy, Beer, Goblet, Liqueur Flute, Liqueur Saucer, Gin, Wine Tumbler, Whiskey Tumbler, Long Drink, Candlestick.

**Suggested Pricing for Monbijou**

NPD

## *Ocular Tumblers*
### Designed by Stuart Garfoot

Molded in and on the glass, a single circular "eye" meets yours as you admire the shape before tasting the drink. Ocular items were made for: Whiskey Old Fashioned, Liqueur, Whiskey Double Old Fashioned, and Long Drink. They were also available in 8" and 9 1/2" bowls as well as vases sized at 9 1/4", 11" and 13 1/2".

### Suggested Pricing for Ocular

$30-$60 each item.

Ocular Tumblers.

# Ophelia

Graceful stemware, formal in concept, Ophelia adds grace to an elegant meal, a sophisticated table. Stemware included: Water, Burgundy, Wine, Champagne Flute and Brandy.

**Suggested Pricing for Ophelia**

$45-$50 each stem.

# Polygon
## Designed by Michael Boehm

Polygon, tall, slim and elegant, has captured the spirit of grace and refinement. The delicately faceted bowl reflects light while the rippled stem adds function to the refined shape. Items include: Water/White Wine, Red Wine, Burgundy, Liqueur, Champagne Flute, 17" Decanter, and a 7" Footed Bowl. Michael Boehm's Polygon clearly sets a high standard.

**Suggested Pricing for Polygon**

$40-$100 each item.

Ophelia

Polygon footed bowl.

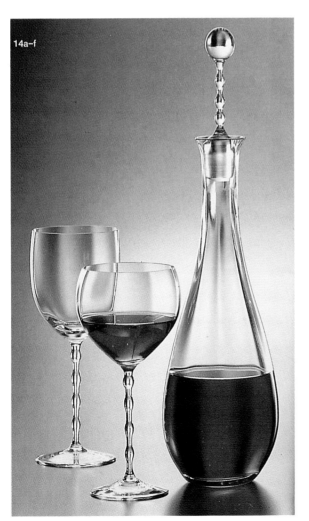

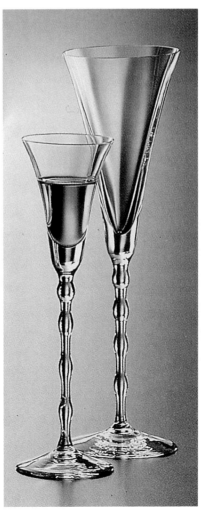

Polygon glasses and decanter.

# Romance

Perfectly executed to accompany the Romance dinnerware, the glass line was made in a patterned Straw Glass series with tall and delicate stems as well as a Chalice Glass series identified by a shorter, footed stem.

Straw items include: Red Wine, Burgundy, White Wine, Liqueur, Liqueur Saucer, Champagne Flute, Saucer Champagne, Beer, Beer Tumbler.

Chalice items include: Port, White Wine, Red Wine, Saucer Champagne, Champagne Flute, Liqueur Flute, Liqueur Saucer, Beer, Beer Tumbler, Goblet, Brandy, Decanter, Jug.

**Suggested Pricing for Romance**

$80-$100 each stem.

Romance Straw Glass series.

Romance Chalice Glass series.

## Single Stems (Collector Flutes)

Late, but very important to emerging styles, these single stems by several designers direct our attention to the finest glass we find (aside from Studio glass work). The items, so finely executed, are the heirlooms of tomorrow, worthy of our attention today. This grouping was so popular that another important selection followed it. Neither group could be considered more important than the other.

**Suggested Pricing for Collector Flutes**

NPD

From left: Black Crown, designed by Nancy Still McKinney; Amulett, designed by Michael Boehm; Volute, designed by Nanny Still McKinney; Birdy, designed by Stuart Garfoot; Yang's Pearls, designed by Yang; Spalier, designed by Laura De Santillana.

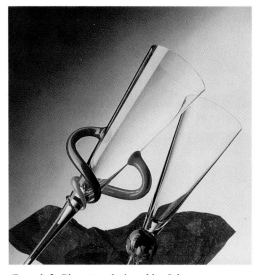

From left: Pirouette, designed by Johan van Loon; Bijou, designed by Barbara Brenner.

From left: Snake Glass, designed by Arlon Bayliss; Helix, designed by Arlon Bayliss; Champagne Fountain, designed by C.J. Riedel; Network, designed by Nanny Still McKinney; Capriole, designed by Michael Boehm; Infini, designed by Rosemonde Nairac; Paradiso, designed by Arlon Bayliss; Carnivale, designed by Michael Boehm.

## Touch 1920

This elegant, graceful design with dragonfly-detailed stems brings the Art Deco style to the table. Light hearted, but strictly executed, Touch 1920 has spoken to many who seek out the best of Rosenthal's crystal designs. Items include: Burgundy, Champagne Flute, Brandy, Sherry, Beer, Liqueur, Water, Saucer Champagne, White Wine. A Decanter, Jug and Candlesticks join the stemware.

**Suggested Pricing for Touch 1920**

$50-$80 each stem.

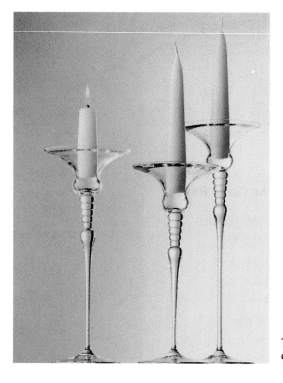

Touch 1920 candlesticks.

Touch 1920 glasses and decanter.

## *Whiskey Tumblers*
### Designed by Bjorn Wiinblad

Firm, steady shapes designed for different uses characterize these tumblers. All were crystal with sham bottoms, in six sizes said to be for six different "on the rocks" drinks.

**Suggested Pricing for Whiskey Tumblers**

$30-$60 each tumbler.

Four of the six different Whiskey Tumblers.

111

# Glass Dinnerware

### *Roman Stripe*
**Designed by Annie Glass**

Roman Stripe brought a new dimension to the traditional porcelain lines which Rosenthal had made. This new handmade pattern brought a sunburst of gold or platinum to the table, balancing it with shapes which allowed the decoration to make its own statement. Another late design, it is important to collectors of Rosenthal since it marks a definite point of change. It was initially offered in a 7" Dessert Pate, 10" Dinner Plate, and a 12" Buffet Plate.

**Suggested Pricing for Roman Stripe**

NPD

# *Decanters*

This Decanter group illustrates the divide that separates Rosenthal's glass production from that of others. These collector decanters, whimsical but elegant, are works of art singularly; when filled with different colored liquids and used in groupings, they represent sophistication at its zenith.

**Suggested Pricing for Decanters**

NPD

Roman Stripe dinnerware.

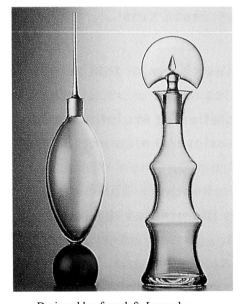

Designed by, from left: Laura de Santillana, Jan van der Vaart.

Designed by Guggisberg/Baldwin.

Designed by, from left: Lino Sabattini, Andreas von Weizsäcker.

Designed by, from left: Michael Boehm, Ambrogio Pozzi, Michael Boehm, Arlon Bayliss, Stuart Garfoot, Stuart Garfoot, Guggisberg/Baldwin.

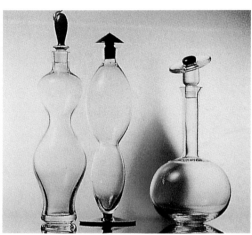

Designed by, from left: Laura de Santillana, Allessandro de Santillana, Nanny Still McKinney.

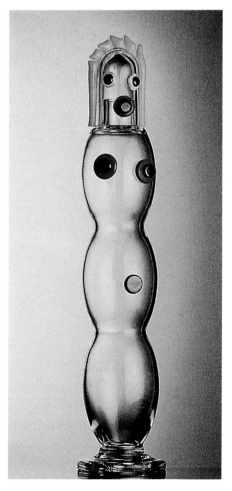

Designed by Ambrogio Pozzi.

113

The Aqualux candleholder.

# Candleholders and Candelabras

## *Aqualux*
### Designed by Timo Sarpaneva and Johannes Dinnebier

Sarpaneva and Dinnebier collaborated on the Aqualux candleholder. It allows a special candle to float in a narrow crystal vase, rising as it burns, the flame always above the water. An arm held the three or five arm candleholder, which was 9 1/2" high.

### Suggested Pricing for Aqualux

Candleholder, 1 arm: $98
Candleholder, 3 arm: $298

## *Flame*
### Designed by Michael Boehm

Flame, another Michael Boehm design, contrasted delicate crystal with the intensity of the flame placed in close proximity to the flame-shaped crystal holder, catching refractions and adding to the candle glow.

### Suggested Pricing for Flame

5" Flame Candleholder: $50-$65

The Flame candleholder.

## *Laura*
### Designed by Laura de Santillana

Laura, a combination of glass and steel in a lavish candlestick flower vase, allows for individual expression when used as an accessory or centerpiece.

**Suggested Pricing for Laura**

NPD

Two views of the Laura candleholder.

## Sparrow

Sparrow candleholders were sculptured small bird figures made of full lead crystal. The surfaces of the figures showed the candlelight as it was reflected in different angles, adding to the attractive quality of the figural pieces. They were designed by the Rosenthal Studio.

**Suggested Pricing for Sparrow**

Candleholder: $30-$40

## Star
### Designed by Vicki Lindstrand

Vicki Lindstrand designed the Star candleholders. They were said to be made of the purist hand-cut full lead crystal. The refraction of these delicate pieces caught the glow from candles, casting shadows and light in unexpected directions. They were available in 1 3/4", 2 1/2", 3 1/2" and 4 3/4" sizes, as well as Hanging Stars which were available in pairs.

**Suggested Pricing for Star**

Candleholders: $33-$100
Hanging Stars: $50-$100

**Above:**
The Sparrow candleholder.

**Right:**
Star candleholders.

117

# Glass Vases, Bowls, and Other Accessories

## Arabesque
### Designed by Nanny Still McKinney

Nanny Still McKinney named a smoking accessory and bowl line Arabesque. Functional in every detail, the pieces broke sameness with curving lines divided by smaller sections of the same lines adding self detail. Plates were 8" and 6 1/4", ashtrays were 4" and 5 1/2", and bowls were 4 3/4", 7", and 9 1/2".

**Suggested Pricing for Arabesque**

Large plate: $100-$200
Bowls: $65-$85
Ash Trays: $55-$65

## Drapery
### Designed by Michael Boehm

Boehm's Drapery vase and bowl are unmistakably exotic adaptations of design, defying balance while achieving dramatic results. The 8 1/2" vase and the bowl both involve an oversized flare of glass, which extends unevenly, literally draping the top of the vase. Drapery was also available in a 16 1/2" bowl.

**Suggested Pricing for Drapery**

NPD

Arabesque bowls.

Drapery bowl and vase.

Arabesque plates.

Arabesque ashtrays.

## Igloo Boxes
### Designed by Sami Wirkkala

Igloo Boxes were round 4 3/4" crystal boxes which could be used in many ways. They were sold as paperweights, candy dishes, ashtrays, jewelry boxes, and more. The two heavy crystal halves combined into a glistening object d'art.

### Suggested Pricing for Igloo Boxes

$75-$100 each piece.

## Marina
### Designed by Jan Adam

Marina seemed a glass from the sea, for its use of color comes in parts as though being carried by water. Using two shades of green it makes the statement which the designer chose, but collectors may recall the design as one suggestive of the old "end of day" style. Jan Adam designed this interesting group of vases and a centerpiece bowl.

### Suggested Pricing for Marina

NPD

## Olympus
### Designed by Michael Boehm

The Olympus line by Michael Boehm is best represented by a stemmed bowl, designed by drawing five threads of the stem from a single drop of molten glass. The 13 1/4" bowl for fruit or flowers is just as elegant when standing alone. The smaller bowl, 11 3/4", is equally fine. The 12" candleholder has a flat bowl arc upon which votive or decorative candles may be placed. Olympus is, clearly, one of Rosenthal's masterpieces in glass.

### Suggested Pricing for Olympus

NPD

Igloo Boxes

Marina vases and centerpiece bowl.

The Olympus stemmed bowl.

119

Nautilus

## *Pan, Tao and Nautilus*
### Designed by Yang

Pan, Tao, and Nautilus, with abstract designs and amorphic shapes, were designed by Yang. Pan was undecorated. Tao is seen with a rhythmic decoration and Nautilus was decorated with golden shells accenting the shapes. They came in vases which were 8 1/2" and 10" tall as well as an 8 1/2" bowl.

### Suggested Pricing for Pan, Tao, and Nautilus

Vases: $300-$400
Bowl: $350-$450

**Left:**
Tao

**Opposite:**
Pan

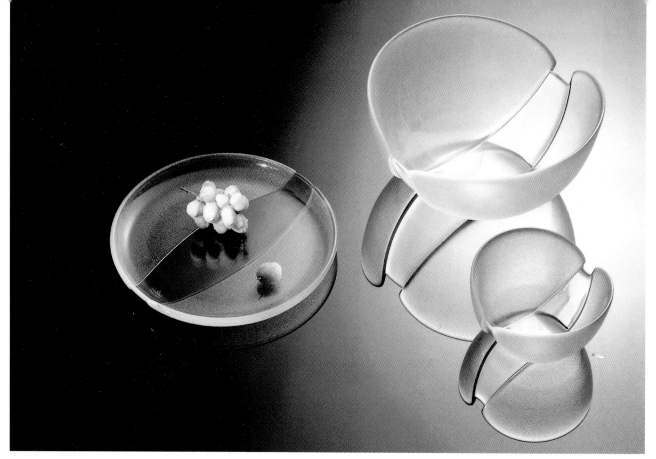

Paso Doble bowls and plate.

## *Paso Doble*
### Designed by Sami Wirkkala

Sami Wirkkala designed the frosted glass Paso Doble bowls. The rounded bowls appear to open, showing a clear glass division. Textural difference combined with unusual shape makes this serving bowl group attractive in any setting.

### Suggested Pricing for Paso Doble

Bowl, 5 1/2": $29
Bowl, 7 1/2": $65
Bowl, 9 1/2": $98
Bowl, 11 1/2": $150
Plate, 6 1/4": $30
Plate, 10 1/4": $65

## *Schnapps Eggs*
### Designed by C. J. Riedel

Schnapps Eggs, sold by pairs, were designed by Professor C. J. Riedel to be roly poly, whimsical, and interesting. The weight swayed on a ring around their center of gravity and they were stabilized only when filled. They fit neatly into Rosenthal's gift line, which was meant to serve informal as well as formal use.

### Suggested Pricing for Schnapps Eggs

Gift box of two: $50-$65

## *Sonara*
### Designed by Laura de Santillana

The Sonara Bowl was made in three bowl sizes: 5 1/2", 8", and 10 1/4", and was accompanied by an 9 1/2" plate. Functional, its wide brim accents the wave self-decoration which is followed to the generous foot. It adds sophistication to any table.

### Suggested Pricing for Sonara

Bowl, 5 1/2": $35-$50
Bowl, 8": $65-$85
Bowl, 10 1/2": $100-$125

Pair of Schnapps Eggs.

122

Sonara bowls and plate.

### Zauberwald
**Designed by Michael Boehm**

This vase line, designed by Boehm, plays the texture of crystal against crystal, producing exciting pieces of lead crystal. The vases were 5 1/2" and 7", small marvels of glass.

**Suggested Pricing for Zauberwald**

NPD

**Zauberwald vase.**

# Colored Crystal

## Beluga
**Designed by Yang**

The primary colors, fashioned by Yang into bowls and vases with striking knob detail and feet that reach out to be grasped. A '90s statement that transcends all the decades of this century.

**Suggested Pricing for Beluga**

NPD

Beluga bowls.

Selection of Colorfire vases.

## Color Fire
**Designed by Michael Boehm**

Michael Boehm took traditional shapes and made unusual glass vases of them. Using variants of a color, he was able to use them to engage attention, clearly an ingredient of his skills. He named the line Color Fire. Vases, which differed in size and color range, included: Blue/Lilac, 6 1/4"; Yellow/Green, 9 1/2"; Red, 11 1/2"; Blue/Green, 12"; and Yellow, 15 3/4".

**Suggested Pricing for Color Fire**

Vases: $225-$325

## Kontiki, Nightlife, and Samoa
**Designed by Nanny Still McKinney**

Nanny Still McKinney designed her bowl/bottle Kontiki shapes in glass using shaded brilliant yellows, red, and greens to draw the eye over each piece, finding interest here, a bit of magic there. Bowls were 6 1/4", 9 1/2", and 8 3/4"; a vase was 9 1/2". A Covered Box and Decanter were included, as were a sherry glass and a wine glass. She also designed Nightlife, candleholders in bright and eye catching colors. McKinney's Samoa vases in yellow, lilac, and red gave dimensional differences to add to the solid colors.

**Suggested Pricing for Kontiki, Nightlife and Samoa**

Kontiki Bowls and Vases: $350-$400
Kontiki Covered box and Decanter: $375
Kontiki Sherry and Wine glasses: $95-$115
Nightlife Candleholders: $98
Samoa Vases: $200-$300

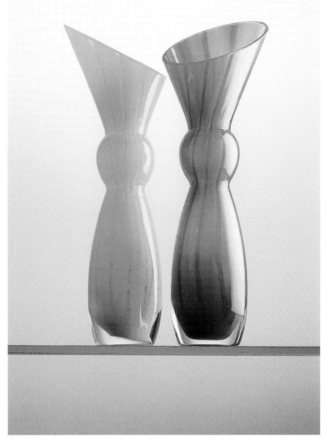

Samoa vases.

**Above and right:**
Selection of Kontiki colored crystal pieces.

Nightlife candleholders.

127

# Gifts and Accessories

The listings and pictures presented here are representative of the early Classic home accessory and gift items which the Rosenthal firm produced from a very early time. Later accessory items and small service groups from the Studio Line are also detailed as it seems helpful to treat this production as a whole.

Early complicated shapes and decorations testify that there was a dedication to excellence from the very beginning of production and we are able to view the evolution of that dedication as the Classic line continues today. The parallel Studio Line items mirror those early standards.

Pricing has not been included for all of the production, as many items are too important to omit even though collector market pricing has not been established. Our listing of early and late production details is abbreviated and readers should understand that these are typical items, not all-inclusive listings. Many seem important to our future collecting, however, and with the advent of estate sales which customarily offer fine quality items, not yet antique, an acquaintance with some of these late lines indicate the potential of this production.

## Early Collections, Accessory Items, and Small Services

### Art Nouveau Vase

This vase, with a river landscape painting colored in pastel colors of gray, green, pink, and violet, dates from 1907 and shows reflective impressions and naturalistic theme in harmony with shape. It is 7 1/4" tall. $75-$100.

**Suggested Pricing for Art Nouveau Vase**

NPD

Art Nouveau
vase.

## Early Vases

Early vases dating from about 1900 are shown here. The first, designed by Kronach, has an octagon body narrowing at the top, coming to a bulbous opening. It is of a green marbleized lustre finish, 6 3/8" tall. Beside it is a lidded vase with a female form decoration on one side, two flying dragons on the other. The wave shaped neck and cover are delicate treatments and the handles are flower stalks with flat gold luster finish. Footed, it has two floral buds as finials and overwrapped handles. It also has a green marbleized finish with lilies and leaves in relief at the base. Measuring 9 5/8" tall, this vase is attributed to Rohring and may be considered a fine example of his work. A floor vase of green marbleized porcelain with allegorical figures in relief dates from 1900. A marbleized flask, 9 7/8" tall, in a lustre glaze, was designed by Kronach. These are good examples of turn of the century styles as executed in fine porcelain, in the private collection of the firm, and donated to the Museum of Art in Berlin.

**Above:**
Two early vases and flask.

**Left:**
Floor vase with allegorical figures.

**Suggested Pricing for Early Vases**

Vase, 6 3/8": $115-$135
Vase, 9 5/8": $145-$200
Floor Vase: $325-$500
Flask: $275-$375

## K'ang-hsi Floor Vase

A floor vase, K'ang-hsi, dates from 1926 and illustrates the use of floral decorations on style typical of the Orient. 30" tall, it is an example of an intricate and complicated pattern on a large scale. Polychromed, mauve, and orchid are the principal colors. It was decorated by Walter Mutze.

**Suggested Pricing for Floor Vase**

$225-$300.

K'ang-hsi vase.

## Espresso Collectors' Sets

A Wildlife Series of eight sets (Cup, Saucer, and Decorated Dessert Plate) emphasizes interest in naturalistic design. This abbreviated list illustrates Rosenthal's continuing interest in this sort of production.

**Suggested Pricing for Espresso Sets**

Cups and Saucers: $115-$135 per set
Dessert Plates: $35-$50

Purple Gallinule motif.

Hummingbird motif.

Tukane motif.

## Artist Collectors' Cup Assortments

Cups and saucers, of several assortments, all quite handsome and all designed with the same care which went into dinnerware lines or individual items, have been very important to collectors. Most were not named beyond the motif number ascribed to them. That number allows us to be certain of the designer. They differ in shape as well as decoration and though many have been in the line for a long time, the assortment is updated with regularity, leaving collectors waiting for just one more! A sampling is shown here.

**Suggested Pricing for Collectors' Cups**

$65-$100

No. 8, designed by James Kirkwood.

No. 30, designed by Jean-Claude de Crousaz.

No. 25, designed by Salomé.

No. 23, designed by Otto Piene.

131

# Ch'ing Dynasty Collection

Pricing applies to all decorations

## Decoration "Blanc De Chine"
**(#000100)**

Tea Caddy, 4": $45-$65
Tea Caddy, 4 3/4": $50-$100
Bowl, 6 1/4": $20-$55
Bowl, 8 1/2": $45-$65
Vase, 6 1/4": $35-$55
Vase, 7" (2 Styles): $40-$60
Vase, 8 1/2" (3 Styles): $45-$85
Vase, 9 1/2" ( 2 Styles): $45-$85
Vase, 10 1/4" (2 Styles): $50-$100
Wall Plate, 8 1/4": $25-$45
Wall Vase, 7 3/4": $45-$70
Wall Vase, 9 1/2": $50-$75
Rice Wine Cup: $25-$45

## Decoration "Landscape"
**(#002317)**

Rice Wine Cup
Vase, 7"
Vase, 8 1/2"
Vase, 10 1/4"

## Decoration "Le Jardin"
**(#002318)**

Lamp, 9 1/2"
Wall Vase, 7 3/4"
Wall Vase, 9 1/2"
Tea Caddy, 4"
Tea Caddy, 4 3/4"
Vase, 6 1/4"
Vase, 8 1/2"
Vase, 9 1/2"

## Decoration "Pheasants"
**(#002319)**

Vase, 7"
Vase, 8 1/2"
Vase, 10 1/4"
Lamp, 10 1/4"

## Decoration "Famille Rose"
**(#002320)**

Lamp, 10 1/4"
Wall Plate, 8 1/4"
Tea Caddy, 4"
Tea Caddy, 4 3/4"

## Decoration "Famille Verte"
**(#002321)**

Vase, 7 3/4"
Vase, 9 1/2"
Vase, 11 3/4"
Lamp, 9 1/2"
Lamp, 11 3/4"

## Decoration "Long Life"
**(#002348)**

Bowl, 7 3/4"

Bowls and vases; "Blanc de Chine" decoration.

Vases and rice wine cup;
"Landscape" decoration.

Wall plate, tea caddies, and lamp; "Le Jardin" decoration.

Vases; "Pheasants" decoration.

Vases; "Famille Rose" decoration.

Vases; "Famille Verte" decoration.

Bowl; "Long Life" decoration.

# Studio Line Accessory Items

Many vase assortments were offered in black or white, some were single items, some architectural in concept, others amorphous, a few whimsical. It is important that we recognize these despite the fact that their numbers are few; they represent real challenge in designs that were not decorated but depended upon surface detail for the important expression they offered. Outstanding decoration work by many of Rosenthal's artists has been done on some of the shapes described in this listing, a selection of which are illustrated here. Becoming acquainted with these shapes enables us to identify and add to the decorations shown here, for it is certain that great shapes will always supply the canvas for fine decoration, regardless of time.

## Cat Lights
### Designed by Otmar Alt

These colorful figurine candlesticks capture primary colors and sculpt them into fanciful cat and kitten pieces. Turned around, they show the cat with a different "attitude." Not "alley cats," these are prize winners, designed by Otmar Alt. The Tabby is 9 1/2" and the Tomcat is 12".

**Suggested Pricing for Cat Lights**

NPD

## Circolo Pozzi and Angolo Ambrogio
### Designed by Ambrogio Pozzi

Ambrogio Pozzi's assortment of small vases were half circles decorated with diamond shapes on a necklace-like arrangement, aptly named Circolo Pozzi, a sculptured vase, beautifully detailed. His Angolo Ambrogio featured footed vases which combined geometric shapes by forming half moon tops with diagonal lines meeting where the foot began, extending to an elevated foot.

**Suggested Pricing for Circolo Pozzi**

White, 3 1/2": $145-$165
Black, 3 1/2": $165-$200

**Suggested Pricing for Angolo Ambrogio**

White, 5 1/2": $160-$200
Black, 7": $175-$225
9 1/2": $225-$250

## Cresta
### Designed by Uta Feyl

Cresta by Uta Feyl contrasts the movement of waves against a ribbed section of the vases. These were also available in bowls and candlesticks. The avant-garde combination is a striking one, calling for dramatic presentation.

**Suggested Pricing for Cresta**

NPD

134

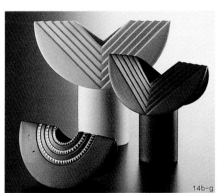

**Above:**
Cat Lights

**Left:**
Circolo Pozzi vase
and two Angolo
Ambrogio vases.

**Right:**
Cresta vases.

**Left:** Debut vases.

**Right:** Gemini vases.

## *Debut*
### Designed by Michael Boehm

Boehm's Debut line, so modern, so well executed, pits oval and square against each other in lines so interesting that they are among the very best of this type of Rosenthal production.

**Suggested Pricing for Debut**

6 1/4": $75-$100
8 1/2": $175-$200
White, 9 1/2": $195-$250
Black, 9 1/2": $225-$265

Filigran vases and bowls.

## *Filigran*
### Designed by Johan Van Loon

A late, but very interesting group of accessory items was named Filigran by the designer Johan Van Loon. The shapes were rhythmic and flowing with parts of each piece showing the pattern which had been cut from the piece in a filigree process. Delicate in weight, size and detail, these are important pieces to collectors.

**Suggested Pricing for Filigran**

Vase, 6 1/2": $180-$215
Vase, 7": $185-$225
Vase, 8 1/2": $200-$250
Bowl, 7": $125-$150
Bowl, 10 1/4": $200-$250
Lantern, 6 1/2": $225-$300

## *Gemini*
### Designed by Lino Sabattini

Gemini Vases by Lino Sabattini seem divided into mirror halves with a clear shaped division. Available in white or black porcelain, these are very fine late examples.

**Suggested Pricing for Gemini**

NPD

## *Giardino*

Giardino, with a naturalistic panel in either black, white, or white with gold, came in several sizes as well as a companion low bowl.

**Suggested Pricing for Giardino**

NPD

Giardino

Graficana vases.

## Graficana
**Designed by Brigitte Doege**

Brigitte Doege designed Graficana items with abstract details of irregular shapes, colored them with sophistication and placed the designs on vases sized 4 3/4", 5 1/2", 7", 8" and 8 1/2". Variations of the pattern are on a 7" Tray and a 12" Bowl. Bright, lively, and colorful, they are typical of the sort of work Ms. Doege does with such skill.

**Suggested Pricing for Graficana**

$95-$200 each item.

## Love Story
**Designed by Bjorn Wiinblad**

Love Story is a small grouping of fantasy figures finely drawn and surrounded by brightly colored birds, all done on various vases. It is so typical of Wiinblad's work that it brings immediate praise from those who are acquainted with it.

**Suggested Pricing for Love Story**

Vase, 7": $185-$225
Pillow Vase: $125-$165
Vase, 4 1/2": $90-$125
Vase, 5 1/2": $90-$125

## Metropolis
**Designed by Yves Galgon**

Yves Galgon has captured the busy life of the city in his Metropolis. Vases and a tray done in abstractions which blend blues or reds form a futuristic selection which has become popular in late production.

**Suggested Pricing for Metropolis**

NPD

## Pollo
**Designed by Tapio Wirkkala**

Tapio Wirkkala, with such impressive dinnerware credentials, brings us also small sculptured pieces which seem to have been with the world forever. His Pollo vase made in two sizes came in black and white, and reflects the light differently each time one looks at it.

**Suggested Pricing for Pollo**

$185-200

Love Story vases and wall plate.

Metropolis vases.

Pollo vases in white and black.

## Purpura
### Designed by Johan van Loon

This futuristic grouping of vases, ashtray and a tray seems to have a wave-like texture of indeterminate detail, interestingly accented with brown and blue, used in a way that adds interest to the texture.

### Suggested Pricing for Purpura

Ash Tray: $75-$100
Vase, 8 1/2": $85-$125
Vase, 9 1/4": $125-$150
Tray, 10 1/2": $140-$165

Purpura ashtray, vases, and tray.

Raja vases.

## Raja

Recalling an Indian world, the Raja group was beautifully decorated in vivid pastels. It included vases in five sizes as well as low bowls.

### Suggested Pricing for Raja

NPD

## Scallops
### Designed by Rosemonde Nairac

This vase assortment by Rosemonde Nairac was given the name Scallops. The white irregular vertical lines are broken high on the vases with rounded ends, clearly suggestive of scallops.

### Suggested Pricing for Scallops

4 1/4": $100-$125
6 1/4": $125-$150
7": $185-$215

Scallops vases.

142

## *Taurus*
### Designed by Jan van der Vaart

Taurus held so much promise that it was offered in full black and white assortments. Jan van der Vaart combined an ovoid shape with a top opening suggestive of a pleat. The effect was dramatic, made even more so when Helmut Drexler decorated it with a "Rose Gold" pattern. The all-over pattern softens the lines with the spectacular rose lustre pattern. Taurus "Springfield" adapted a bold color contrasting floral pattern, bringing informality and warmth to the shape. Maarten Vrolijk gives us this different application.

### Suggested Pricing for Taurus
Add 50 percent for black, 100 percent for most decorations.

Vase, 6 1/4": $149
Vase, 8": $249
Vase, 9 1/2": $299
Vase, 11": $395
Bowl, 7 3/4": NPD

Vases and bowl in Taurus "Springfield."

## *Triga Notturno*
### Designed by Jane Osborn-Smith and Yang

A grouping for three vases and a low bowl is said to have been based on a trigonometric design, with colorful contrasting detail below vertical lines which extend to the opening of the vase. The grouping is a collaboration by Osborn-Smith and the Indonesian artist Yang.

### Suggested Pricing for Triga Notturno

NPD

Triga Notturno

## *Recent Artist Espresso Cups*

These cups, two of which are shown here, are done on the Cupola shape. They are a smaller line, though some come with a cream jug and sugar bowl. They also form an open-ended collection, with international designers competing for the most fitting cafe design.

### Suggested Pricing for Artist Espresso Cups

NPD

Espresso Cup No. 16, designed by Sami Wirkkala.

143

Espresso Cup No. 2, designed by Barbara Brenner.

Espresso Cup No. 15, designed by Gilbert Portanier.

## *Recent Mythos Espresso Cups*

The Mythos espresso cups are fewer, the line younger, but they are just as sought after as are the other cup collections. Bright bird's wing handles define the shapes of this popular group.

**Suggested Pricing for Mythos Espresso Cups**

NPD

Mythos Cup No. 6, designed by Jane Osborn-Smith.

Mythos Cup No. 1, designed by Bjorn Wiinblad.

Mythos Cup No. 4, designed by Yang.

144

# Parchment Porcelain

These delicate, fragile accessory items were designed by Johan van Loon. Simple and functional in shape, with the only added decoration the use of subtle color, they are typical of most of the work which van Loon did for the Rosenthal company. He shaped this important porcelain by flattening it with a rolling pin before molding. In such a manner, thin-walled, exquisitely sculptured shapes evolve. Light, almost to the point of transparency, allows for the interplay of shadow with light. Sierra, one of van Loon's most detailed shapes, adds colored textural features to the dramatic lines which we find in his other designs. Most of this work adapts itself to vases, all directly reflecting the sophistication of simplicity, some incorporating color in minimal amounts. Juror comments tell us that "Johan van Loon's designs are of extreme intricacy and can be realized in practice only by means of an unusually high standard of manufacture. It is for this very reason that van Loon's work is without parallel in contemporary industrial design." The esthetic quality of these designs disguise the fact that they are factory made, for they have the appearance of studio pottery at its finest.

**Suggested Pricing for Parchment Porcelain**

NPD

 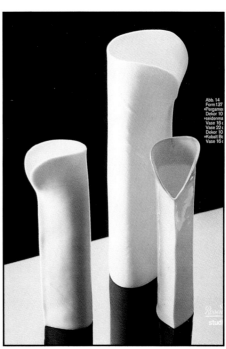

Parchment porcelain vases.

Johan van Loon's
"Sierra" vases.

145

# Titania and Moliere Ivory

## Titania

### Suggested Pricing for Titania

Add 100 percent for "Heron," "Portugal Rose," "Audubon." Add 200 percent for "Midsummer's Night's Dream," "Enchanted Garden."

Vase, 7": $75
Vase, 7 3/4" (2 Styles): $80
Vase, 17": $150
Vase, 8 1/2": $85
Vase, 9 1/4" (2 Styles): $95
Vase, 11" $100
Vase, 11 3/4" (1 Handle): $135

Vase, 12 1/2" (2 Styles): $125
Vase, 14" (2 Handles): $165
Vase, 15 1/2": $175
Vase, 17": $200
Vase, 19" (Floor): $300
Covered Vase, 12 1/2": $145
Covered Vase, 14 3/4": $155

Footed Tray, 8 1/2": $60
Footed Tray, 11 3/4": $75
Covered Box: $45
Tray, 8 1/2": $55
Small Tray, 4": $45
Chop Dish, 13": $80
Candy Tray, 4": $40

Titania covered box and trays in White.

Titania vases, tray, and chopdish in "Portugal Rose."

Titania vases and footed trays in "Midsummer Night's Dream."

Titania flower pots in "Heron."

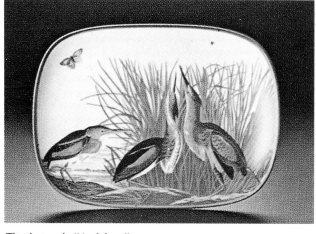

Titania tray in "Audubon."

Titania vases, chopdish, and
trays in "Enchanted Garden."

# *Moliere Ivory*

## Suggested Pricing for Moliere Ivory

Moss Rose, all items; Antiquity and Arcadia, asterisked (*) items only. No vases were made in the Arcadia Decoration.

Tray, 4": $35-$50
Tray, 5 3/4"*: $45-$60
Tray, 6 1/4"*: $50-$70
Tray, 7"*: $50-$65
Fruit Dish, 7 3/4"*: $40-$55
Fruit Dish, 9"*: $45-$55
Footed Fruit, 6 3/4"*: $55-$65
Footed Fruit, 7 1/2"*: $65-$75
Cake Plate*: $85-$115
Vase, 4 3/4": $35-$50
Vase, 5 3/4"*: $50-$60
Vase, 7" (Candleholder)*: $80-$100
Vase, 9 1/2": $75-$115
Vase, 13 1/2": $85-$125
Ash Tray: $22-$30
Small Tray, Round, 4": $35-$45
Small Tray, Round with Scalloped Edge, 4": $40-$50
Cigarette Holder: $30
Candleholder: $32
Covered Box: $38

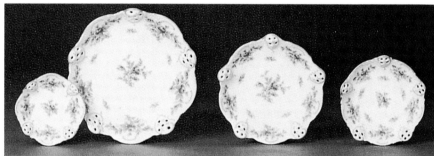

Moliere Ivory cake plate and trays in "Moss Rose."

Moliere Ivory fruit dishes in "Arcadia."

Moliere Ivory cake plate and tray in "Antiquity.'

# Avant-Garde Accessories

## Alta Mira and Liguria
**Designed by Gilbert Portanier**

The French artist Gilbert Portanier reached into the past, looking back to man's earliest forms of expression in these designs. Strong colors and ancient forms on vases, footed bowls, bowls, and candlesticks, each with a different application of the design make for an unusual assortment. Portanier called it Alta Mira. Taking a longer step, he designed Liguria, a rich contrast of color and gold on a dark blue ground. It evidences Indian abstractions with the intricate detail usually reserved for those masters of the Renaissance.

**Suggested Pricing for Alta Mira and Liguria**

Add 100 percent for Liguria.

Footed Bowl, 7": $115
Footed Bowl, 11": $300
Bowl, 8 1/2": $150
Bowl, 11": $165
Vase, 4": $55
Vase, 5": $75
Vase, 8": $125
Vase, 10 1/2": $145
Candleholder: $85

Alta Mira bowls, vases, and candleholder.

Liguria bowls, vases, and candleholder.

## Brown Bag and White Bag
**Designed by Tapio Wirkkala**

We should not be surprised that Tapio Wirkkala found beauty in unexpected places. His Brown Bag group realistically illustrates that beauty. A later White Paper Bag group was made in the same sizes and is valued at about $10 higher than the Brown Bag series

**Suggested Pricing for Brown Bag**

4": $59-$65
5 1/2": $79-$85
7": $89-$100

Brown Bag and White Bag vases.

## Dorothy Hafner

Dorothy Hafner's Studio Line gift work is as interesting to modernists as were her dinnerware lines. That she divided this gift work into three divisions amounts to more than good luck for those who seek out examples of her work. "Broadway," a pastel diagonal pattern of various colors is the more restrained of the group, but it makes a strong statement. "Manhattan," whimsical with various bands of squiggles and darts, all of varying widths, colors, and detail, all rhythmic and bold, is certain to delight Hafner collectors. The "New York" group, equally interesting, consisted of vases in a geometric decoration, suggesting the flash of color and beat of windows from which one can view the vibrancy of the city. All of these Hafner items are executed in pastel shades, setting them apart, in color, from her dinnerware lines.

**Suggested Pricing for Broadway**

Vase, 8": $185-$215
Vase, 5 1/2": $150-$185
Tray, 8": $200-$300

**Suggested Pricing for Manhattan**

Vase, 9 1/4": $235-$300
Vase, 4 1/2": $135-175
Vase, 8": $200-$250

**Suggested Pricing for New York**

Vase, 8": $250-$315
Vase, 9 1/4": $325-$450
Vase, 5 1/2": $160-$200
Vase, 7": $200-$300

## Madura Sarong
**Designed by Yang**

Yang added dimension to the pieces which he named Madura Sarong. The design was molded out from the body in a star-like configuration, with black and gold contrasted against the deep blue of the pieces.

**Suggested Pricing for Madura Sarong**

Vases: $150-$300
Tray: $95-$145
Candlesticks: $175-$225

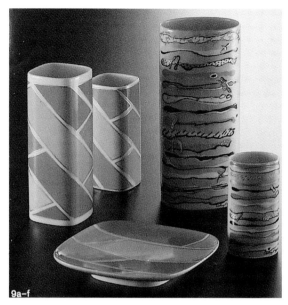

Left: "Broadway" vases and tray.
Right: "Manhattan" vases.

"New York" vases.

Madura Sarong vases.

## Scheherazade/1001 Nights
### Designed by Bjorn Wiinblad

Bjorn Wiinblad plumbs the depth he reached in Magic Flute dinnerware and allows us another look into his fascinating imagination with the gift items he named Scheherazade/1001 Nights. Richly decorated, and all showing Persian influence, the 1001 Nights items are whimsical designs done on a cobalt blue background. No two are decorated with the same characters, the same presentation. Rich in color, the line captures the romanticism of the Rubyiat and continues to engage our attention in all of the decorations which Wiinblad adapted to the theme. It stands out as one of Wiinblad's most important decorations. The 1001 Nights group begins as Sinbad meets the Whale and then embarks upon his adventure which is peopled with fantasy, the mirage world into which Wiinblad steps to find beauty in a land of illusion. This line, with its elegant gold detail, takes us to a dream world of Oriental sights, peopled with some of Wiinblad's most interesting characters. He chose alternate decorations, much the same but differing in contrast. These include "Samuramat," which was a white porcelain with silver design. "Samuramat Black" was highlighted with a gold treatment, and "Duo" was resplendent with color on white. "Quatre Couleurs" with a black background, combined gold and black. "Osiris" showed a golden god, "Chinese Poetry" depicted colorful figures on gold, and "Nutcracker" featured colorful figures on black.

The theme of these fantasy decorations have made this a very popular line. Stemware, equally elegant, was designed with golden dancers on the base and rhythmic swirled bowls. With few established prices available, collectors will recognize that these are very special pieces, considered by some to be among Wiinblad's finest works.

### Suggested Pricing for 1001 Nights

Vase, 7": $300-$400
Vase, 8 1/2": $400-$500
Tray, 8 3/4": $200-$300

"1001 Nights"

"Chinese Poetry"

"Samuramat," shown
in White and Black.

# Bobbles and Bells

Yearly offerings of holiday ornaments have been part of Rosenthal's seasonal line for many years. The classic ornaments shown here center around Renaissance themes, Art Deco influences, and richly detailed influences typical of India, Persia, Nepal, and Arabia. All are enameled in bright colors, profusely accented with gold. They customarily come out as the New Year begins, decorated with a traditional design from another land, another time. Those shown here are typical of those introduced each year.

**Suggested Pricing for Bobbles and Bells**

$45-60

Two examples of holiday bobbles and bells.

# Figurines

## *Representative Figural Pieces*

Early figural pieces can all be considered as rare and difficult to price. Pricing consultants agreed that experience in comparison pricing is limited. The less complicated items may be considered to be worth as much as $400, with many detailed items considerably higher.

"Spanish Dancer," designed by Ferdinand Liebermann in 1910. 7 5/8" tall.

"Snake Dancer" was designed by Rudolf Marcuse in 1917 and made for only one year. Her turning motion allows her garment to form a snake. Blue, brown, and green with gold detail and 15 3/4" tall, this is one of the most collectible of the early works.

"Temple Dedication." Made from 1919 until 1929, this Oriental figurine carries a lantern . Her garment is polychromed with rich ornamental design and much gold accent. She is 13 3/8" tall.

"Korean Dancer," 1919.

"Oriental Figure With Lantern," 1919.

"Two Princesses" shows a girl with crown sitting as if speaking to a goose which is also crowned. Her gown is bright blue and green, with gold detail throughout the figure. Ferdinand Liebermann designed her in 1919 and she was part of the figural line until 1927.

"Foo Dog." The 7 1/4" Foo Dog decorated in blue, green, black, and polished gold has a small dog at its feet It dates from 1927 and was designed by Grete Kramer. It was part of the line until 1929.

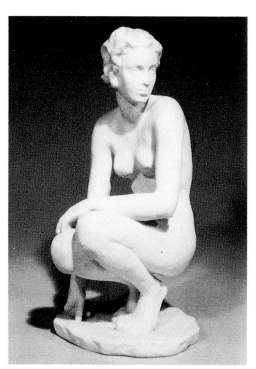

"Croucher" is 14 1/2" tall, made of bisque porcelain, and undecorated This nude was designed by Fritz Klimsch in 1935 and it continued to be part of the line until 1940.

"Autumn" is an Art Deco designed female figure designed by Gerhard Schliepstein in 1928. With a harvest of fruit in her hand, she is undecorated, but the base is inscribed with the words "50 Years of Rosenthal Porcelain," indicating that this is an early advertising piece.

"High School." Designed by
Ferdinand Liebermann, 1910.

"Latin," designed by Ferdinand Liebermann in
1911, shows a man in conversation with a parrot
while another sits on his shoulder.

"Charged Dancer," 9" tall and designed by Berthold
Boehs, dates from 1913 and was produced until 1929.
A dancer, with her toe arched over a round base, arm
to her shoulder, allows her long skirt to flow.

"Frog King" was designed by Leo Rauth in 1914 and
shows a girl enchanted by a frog, also wearing a crown.
With a blue dress and gold detail this measures 4 3/8".

**Left:**
"Teddy School," a 3 5/8" figure of a girl pointing to a book as she teaches Teddy Bears which are seated before her. Her dress is blue.

**Below left:**
"Spring Love" groups a nude woman and man embracing. 9 1/2" tall, this group was designed in 1914 by Richard Aigner. It continued in production until 1917.

**Below:**
"Duet," a tall 13 3/8" Pierrot guitar player is shown sitting on a bank of earth. Rudolf Marcuse designed this in 1913. Gray, green, and black accent the white of the figure's clothing.

"Turtle News" shows the child Bacchus sitting on a turtle playing a flute. With gold detail, this piece was designed by Ferdinand Liebermann and was produced from 1913-1920.

"Guided Flight" illustrates a child riding on the back of a giant winged insect. A. Caasmann designed this 3 5/8" tall figure in 1914 and it was made until 1928.

"Cabaret" is a figural young lady standing on a round base as if in a dancing position as she plays a lute, her dress swirling about her. 16 3/8" tall, she is one of the largest of the early figurines, was designed by Rudolf Marcuse in 1913, and continued in production until 1920.

"Happy March," introduced in 1919 and in production until 1930, features a Pierrette playing the lute with a drum at his feet. Blue and a gray-brown add to this colorful 14 1/2" tall figure designed by C. Holzer-Defanti.

"Pearl Seeker" shows a nude woman kneeling with a large clam shell, examining pearls which are at her feet. She is 10 1/8" tall and was designed by Karl Himmelstoss in 1917.

"Grape Carrier," a colorful figure with blue, brown, and green accented by gold shows a girl with extended arms as if offering a bowl of grapes. She was designed by Rudolf Marcuse in 1917.

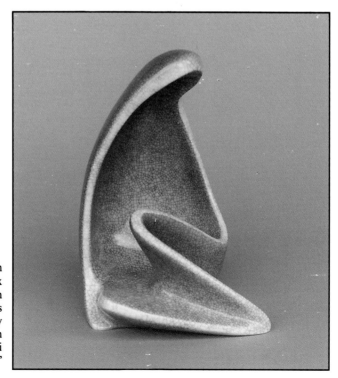

A very "Modern Madonna" with a grey cracked glaze is 9 1/2" x 6". Abstract, she depends upon form for decoration. This piece is signed with the customary signature, but a paper label is in place which includes "Via Strozzi 1 Firenze, Latovola moderna."

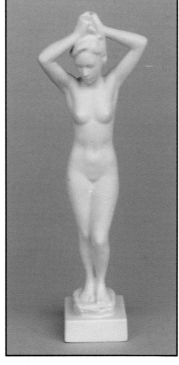

A graceful standing
nude arranging her
hair is 10 1/2" high.
Signed R.M. Werner.

"Nefertiti," still part
of the classic line,
remains popular. It
shows the head of
the Egyptian queen
as we have come to
be familiar with it,
but Rosenthal has
used gloss and
bisque combined to
give detail to the
white porcelain.

"Goat Girl." Very early nude, 7 1/2" tall. Signed M.
Hermfritz, it is believed to date from 1910-1920.

"Snake Charmer," 7 1/2" tall. This bisque porcelain
piece is undecorated except for gold tracings to
highlight the figure, her dress, and the small snake
at her feet. This is believed to be part of the series
which included the Fairy Queen.

# *Classic Figurines*

The following figurines are
all hand painted, unless noted.

"Standing Cat," Professor
Karner. 4" x 4 1/2".

"Empire Dancer," E.V. Langenmantel,
hand painted over glaze. 6 1/2".

"Huntress," Meisel, hand
painted over glaze. 8" x 3 1/2".

"Hunter," Meisel, hand painted
over glaze. 8" x 3 1/2".

"Playing Stallions,"
Meisel, 16 1/4" x
15 1/2".

"Playing Terns," Meisel. 17 1/2" x 12".

"Flamingo," G. Oppelt. 12".

**Left:**
"Baroque Rider," Meisel.
17 1/2" x 14 1/2".

**Below:**
"Squabbling Finches,"
Meisel, hand painted
underglaze. 11".

**Above:**
"Dachshund," Professor Karner,
hand painted underglaze. 4" x 7".
**Left:**
"Stallion," Meisel.

"Game Cock," Professor Jul. Feldtmann,
hand painted underglaze. 5 3/4" x 8".

"Dachshund, begging," Professor Karner,
hand painted underglaze. 9 1/4".

"Kitten, sitting,"
Professor Karner,
hand painted
underglaze. 4 1/2".

"Small Poodle,"
Professor Karner,
hand painted
underglaze. 7" x 8".

"Borzoi Group," M.H. Fritz. 11" x 24".

"Silver Heron," M.H. Fritz,
hand painted underglaze. 10".

"Horse, jumping," Legat. 10" x 9 3/4".

"Horse," Professor Karner, hand painted underglaze. 11 3/4" x 15 1/2".

"King Frederick," Professor Tuaillon, hand painted over glaze. 11 3/4" x 9 3/4".

"Lady with Borzoi," G. Oppelt, hand painted over glaze. 11 1/4" x 7".

"Koala Bear Group," Lilli Kerzinger-Wert, hand painted underglaze. 11".

"Contemplation," Professor Fritz Klimsch,
all ivory bisque. 12", 13 1/2", 16".

"Bird of Paradise," Frutz Geudebreucg,
hand painted over glaze. 18 1/4".

"Girl Reclining," Professor Fritz Klimsch,
ivory bisque. 7 1/4" x 13 1/2".

"Girl Sitting," Professor Fritz
Klimsch, ivory bisque. 9 3/4".

"Sitting Maiden," Schievelbein,
ivory bisque. 5".

"Trotter, Hannibal," Professor Hufmann, ivory
bisque. 10 1/2" x 17 1/2", 12 1/2" x 20 1/4".

"Lillian Harvey," L. Friedrich Gronau,
hand painted over glaze. 11 3/4".

"Scalare Group," Fritz Heidenreich,
hand painted underglaze. 14 1/2".

"Irish Setter," Fritz Heidenreich,
hand painted underglaze. 7 1/2".

"Kingfisher," Fritz Heidenreich, hand
painted underglaze. 5 3/4" x 6 1/2".

"Mallard," Fritz Heidenreich,
ivory bisque. 7 1/2" x 12 3/4".

"Ara, Red and Green," Fritz Heidenreich, hand painted over glaze. 14".

"Fantail Group," Fritz Heidenreich, hand painted over glaze. 19" x 9 3/4".

"Fantail, Single," Fritz Heidenreich, while or hand painted over glaze. 10".

"Horse head, Lippizaner," Professor Hufmann, ivory bisque, wooden base. 17 1/2".

"Wood Grouse," Fritz
Heidenreich, hand painted
underglaze. 6 1/2" x 6 1/4".

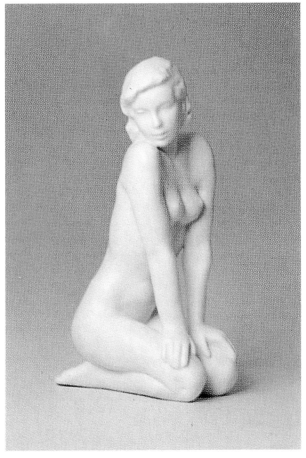

"Girl Kneeling," L. Friedrich-
Gronau, ivory bisque. 8".

"Marianne Simson," L. Friedrich-Gronau,
hand painted over glaze. 11 1/4".

**Above left:**
"Eagle," Fritz Heidenreich, hand painted underglaze. 14 1/2" x 15 1/4".

**Above:**
"Blue Jay," Fritz Heidenreich, hand painted underglaze. 11".

**Left:**
"Ballerina," L. Friedrich-Gronau, hand painted over glaze in rich or light colors. 10".

"Finch of Paradise," Fritz Heidenreich, hand painted over glaze. 9 1/4".

"On the Sea Beach," L. Friedrich-Gronau, ivory bisque. 8 1/2".

"Dachshund," Fritz Heidenreich, hand painted underglaze. 4 1/4" x 8".

"Butterfly," Karl Himmelstof, hand painted over glaze. 1 1/2" x 4".

"Song of the Night,"
Professor W. Fritsch,
white glaze. 11" x 10".

"Lion Group," Fritz Heidenreich, hand
painted underglaze. 6 1/2" x 11".

"The Prophet,"
Professor W. Fritsch,
white glaze. 16 1/4".

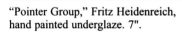

"Snow White," L. Friedrich-Gronau, hand painted over glaze. 9 3/4".

"Pointer Group," Fritz Heidenreich, hand painted underglaze. 7".

**Above:**
"Flamingo Group," Fritz Heidenreich, hand painted over glaze. 13 1/2" x 13 1/2".

**Left:**
"Kitten, playing," Professor Karner, hand painted underglaze. 4 1/4".

"Silver Heron," M.H. Fritz,
hand painted underglaze. 12".

"Heron," Meisel, hand painted
underglaze. 13 1/4".

"Rogue," Forster, hand
painted over glaze. 5 1/2".

"Masquerade," Forster, hand
painted over glaze. 5 1/2".

"Comedian," Forster, hand
painted over glaze. 5 1/2".

"Antelope," Aldo Falchi, hand
painted underglaze. 6 1/2" x 7 1/2".

"Rendezvous Candleholder," Aldo Falchi,
white glaze or hand painted over glaze. 9".

"Panther," Aldo Falchi, hand painted
underglaze. 5 3/4" x 13 1/2".

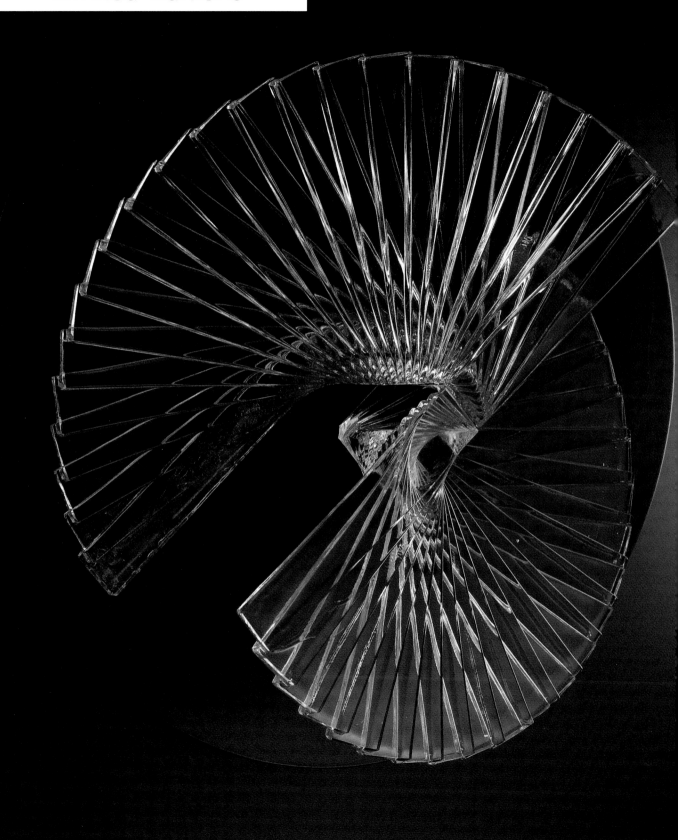

"Torso," a metal sculpture suggesting a link in a chain, is still very much like an abstract torso. 50 pieces of this were made.

Martin Matschinsky and Brigitte Denninghoff designed "Blütenbaum," creating this Baroque centerpiece in a cluster of flowers with naturalistic as well as artistic shapes. Using pure white porcelain, this handsome grouping was limited to 50 pieces.

**Opposite:**
Herbert Bayer's "Glass Winding Stairs" is similar in concept to his great sculptures *The Circular Stairs* in Mexico City and *The Double Ascension* in Los Angeles. Using underlying principles of geometric order and harmony these steps are further emphasized by the reflecting light of the glass. Limited to 150 pieces.

**Above:**
"Onda Construtta," sometimes referred to as "Wave," illustrates the artist's concept of a wave shortly before it breaks. It is a sculpture in motion, a porcelain object achieved with great skill. 100 of these were made.

Left: 150 pieces of "Ellipsoid" by Paul Wunderlich were made. The piece incorporates porcelain, gold-plated bronze, and hand blown glass. It has been described as a piece of "strong, spiritual expressiveness." Above: Wunderlich also designed "Anubis," a figure named after an Egyptian mythological creature. The item was limited to 100 pieces.

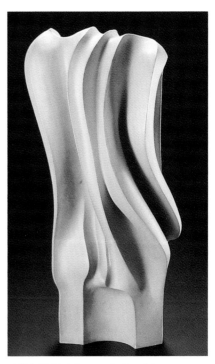

The ceramic works "Quader" (left) and "Idol" (right) were designed by Carlo Zauli and remind one of naturalistic concepts. Sculpturally designed, their surfaces seem to have been derived from the sun, wind, and water. With visual appeal, they also invite the touch. "Quader" was limited to 50 pieces while only 100 pieces of "Idol" were made.

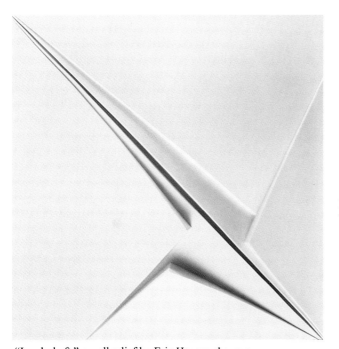

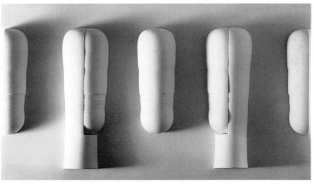

For "Relief 1967," Joannis Avramidis combined three head shapes, reduced to their stereometric fundamental elements. Only 50 pieces were made.

"Landschaft," a wall relief by Eric Hauser, shows a surface tension with complex folding slashed by a stark cut. This ceramic sculpture was limited to 100 pieces.

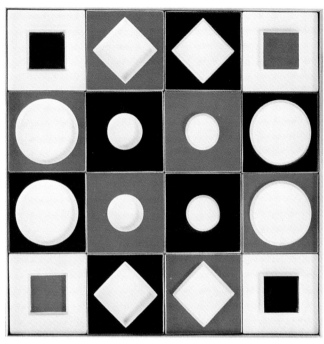

Another wall relief, one of thirteen which Vasarely created for Rosenthal, all of which used basic geometric elements. Different optical effects were achieved on each by the use of different colors and different arrangements of the geometric figures. 75 pieces of this relief were made.

"Colorpath," a wall relief by O. H. Hajek leads the eye across a blue path into an abstract model of a town square. The pieces were limited to 100.

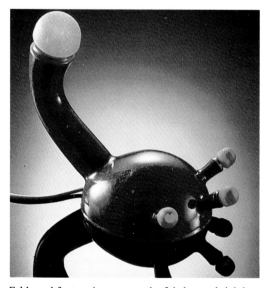

Fable and fantasy in strange, playful shapes, brightly colored, combine in the lamp "Laternentier," which Otmar Alt offered. Avant-garde, it adapts itself to a new use. The production was limited to 100 pieces.

The relief, "Drei Torso" is a block-like concept of the body. In unglazed porcelain, only 50 of these wall reliefs were made. Fritz Wotruba designed them.

The glass "Pegasus," designed by Ernst Fuchs, revives old myths, showing their validity to the present. Pegasus, the winged horse, is detailed in matt smoked glass which heightened the sculptured effect of the relief. 3000 pieces of these plates were made.

"Messenger from Heaven," sometimes referred to as "Heavenly Messenger," was designed by Salvador Dali, who said this work was "inspired by the divine concept of Art, the heavenly messenger guides the snail creature in order to overcome the endless sea of the conventional." The edition was for 2000 pieces.

Michael Boehm designed "Reticelli" glasses which represented the finest glass work that Rosenthal produced. "Reticelli" was named after the white filament ornamentation used by the Murano glass masters in the sixteenth century. Boehm, recognizing that these glasses are very valuable museum pieces, developed a new method for achieving the effect and used it as a basis for his "Reticelli." Several stemmed pieces as well as a bowl were made. The stems were limited to 300 pieces of each size, but only 200 bowls were made.

The porcelain line "Tissu" is aptly described by its name. Very delicate filigree work, made possible by methods especially developed, uses a tissue thin porcelain for the shape. The filigree is carved out of this thin body, further adding to the light and delicate appearance. Alan Whittaker designed "Tissu" and limited the edition to 500 pieces of each of three shapes.

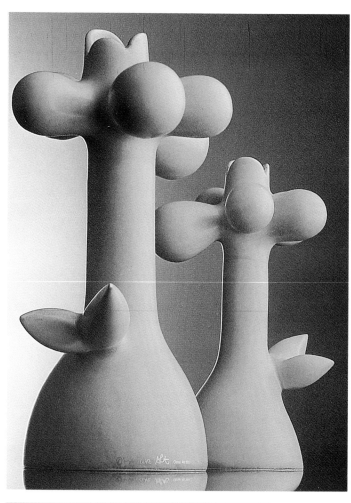

**Above and right:** Otmar Alt designed an object group which he called "Circus." Two vases depict the wild figures of fairy tales and comic strips; 500 of each were made. His "Moon Flower" candleholder is derived from the plant world and the observer is left to interpret the design for himself. The edition was limited to 500 pieces.

A tea set, which Ernst Fuchs named "Zaubersee," was limited to 500 15-piece sets. It was available in white or light blue coloring. Fuchs saw the objects of the sets as suggesting swans and other water creatures.

A relief, appropriately named "Relief Block," was done by Bernhard Heiliger in 1968 in porcelain which was gilded. Limited to 75 pieces.

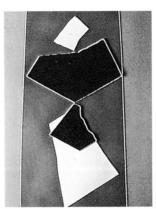

"The Sorceress" was made of green porcelain in 1976. There were 25 made.

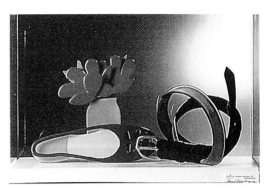

"Still Life," a ceramic treatment was made by Tom Wesselmann in 1982. A manufacturer's unsigned copy was added to the 25 that were made.

The artist Salomé has given us a tigerman or a man-tiger ready to spring to a start. "Tigerman" asks questions, and most would respond.

"Hermes," a Greek god, was to have carried messages from Olympus and shown the dead their way into a new life. Otmar Alt gives us his clown-like tomcat and called him by his Greek name.

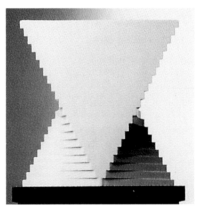

Marcello Morandini gracefully shows the step-by-step construction of a tetra-hedra. Light and dark play against each other in the shadows of the porcelain. The piece was named "Empora."

**Next page:**
Sandro Chia's "Seated Figure" calls attention to carvings that take on the flavor of Etruscan carvings. The figure is expressive and majestic in detail.

The central theme of masks, so important in art and literature, has not been ignored by those whose work is recent. "Pallas Athene," the goddess of wisdom, is done in ceramic by Gilbert Portanier.

Otmar Alt's "Fraulein Maske" shows the face of a cat with features masked behind the face of a child.

"Head," by Janos Kass, combines sculptural and scriptural elements. Writing around the head is from Goethe's "Maxims and Reflections."

## Suomi Limited Art Collection

HAP Grieshaber, using the Suomi shape identified in the dinnerware section, decorated pieces of it with black and platinum, adding to a graphic effect. Signed by the artist, the edition of 500 pieces sold out very quickly.

Objects from the Suomi line were decorated in four different designs by Victor Vasarely. The designs are based on bringing the table objects to a new art form. 500 pieces of each of the four designs were made.

Salvador Dali used the Suomi shape as canvas for his work also. The pieces were given a rich polished gold background and the abstract relief was as futuristic as only Dali would conceive. This edition was popular from the first and the 500 pieces in which it was made sold out very quickly to serious art collectors.

Another decoration on the Suomi shape was done by Ivan Rabuzin. He used delicate, muted colors achieving a pleasant, informal result with oversized flowers and circular clouds. Several shades of blue, touched and accented with gold, decorated 500 pieces.

Eduardo Paolozzi took the micro world of technology and adapted a circuit from a computer, accenting it with subtle colors of pinks and blues against the black background of the Suomi shape. The edition was limited to 500 pieces.

Also limited to 500 pieces was the design which Otto Piene did on four objects from the Suomi line. Surface relief depicting a radiant sun reflected gold and silver accents. Piene used the Tea Pot, Coffee Pot, Covered Vegetable Bowl, and the Salad Bowl for this decoration. 500 pieces of each were made.

Ernst Fuchs, using the same pieces, drew from his stage experience and created designs for the Suomi line using four Lohengrin motifs. Each was placed on the white porcelain, using colorful painted decorations. The edition was limited to 500 pieces.

The Suomi shape was decorated in a "Carmina Burana" design by HAP Grieshaber. He has said that he was inspired by the vagabond songs of the middle ages with their lusty texts of love and nature. Grieshaber selected some of the most beautiful themes from the "Carmine Burana" Oratorio, transferring them to the porcelain shape. 500 pieces were made.

Suomi decoration by HAP Grieshaber.

Suomi decoration by Victor Vasarely.

Suomi decoration by Salvador Dali.     Suomi decoration by Ivan Rabuzin.

Suomi decoration by Eduardo Paolozzi.

Suomi decoration by Otto Piene.

Suomi decoration by Ernst Fuchs.

"Carmina Burana"
decoration on Suomi,
by HAP Grieshaber.

# Appendix: Dinnerware and Cutlery Shapes

## Dinnerware Shapes

### Aida

Dinner Plate, 10¼"
Salad Plate, 7 ½"
B & B Plate, 5 ¾"
Salad Plate, 7 ½"

Tea Cup, #4 low, 6 oz.
Saucer, #4 low

Coffee Cup, #3 high, 6 oz.
Saucer, #3 high

A. D. Cup, #2 high, 3oz.
A. D. Saucer, #2 high

Turkish Cup, #1 high, 3 oz.
Turkish Saucer, #1 high

Rim Soup, 8 ¼"

Fruit, 4 ¼"

Creamsoup Cup, 8 ½ oz.
Creamsoup Saucer

Tureen, 81 oz.

Covered Vegetable, 54 oz.

Sauceboat, 14 ½ oz., 1 pc.

Open Vegetable, #3 med., 51 oz.

Cake Plate
Sandwich Tray
Oval Platter, 15"
Oval Platter, 13"

Salt Shaker
Pepper Shaker

Coffeepot, #3, 44 oz.
A.D. Coffeepot, #1, 20 oz.

Teapot, #3, 37 oz.

Sugar Bowl #3, 11 3/4 oz.
A.D. Sugar Bowl, #1, 5 oz.

Creamer, #3, 11 oz.
A.D. Creamer, #1, 4 oz.

Covered Butter Dish

### Asymmetria

Dinner Plate, 10 ½ "
Salad/Dessert Plate, 8"
B & B Plate, 6"

Service Plate, 12"
Service Plate, 12"

Cup, #4 low
Saucer

Fruit

Rim Soup

Creamsoup Cup
Creamsoup Saucer

Open Vegetable, Small
Open Vegetable, Large

Soup Tureen
Covered Vegetable Bowl

Sauceboat

Platter, 13"
Platter, 15"

Coffeepot

Teapot

Warmer

Creamer

Covered Sugar

Salt
Pepper

After Dinner Cup
After Dinner Saucer

Cake Plate

### Avenue

Dinner Plate, 10 ½"
Salad/Dessert Plate, 8 ½"
B & B Plate, 7"
Service Plate, 12"

Cup, #2 high
Saucer, #2 high

Rim Soup

Fruit Dish

Creamsoup Cup
Creamsoup Saucer

Soup Tureen
Covered Vegetable Bowl

Sauceboat

Open Vegetable 1
Open Vegetable 2

Platter round flat 12"

Platter, 13"
Platter, 15"

Coffeepot

Teapot

Sugar Bowl

Creamer

## Century

 Dinner Plate, 10 ¼"
Salad/Dessert Plate, 8"
B & B Plate, 6 ¼"

 Service Plate/Cake Plate

 Cup, #4 low
Saucer

 Fruit, 4 ¾"

 Coupe Soup, 6 ¾"

 Creamsoup Cup
Creamsoup Saucer

 Open Vegetable, Small
Open Vegetable, Large

 Covered Vegetable Bowl

 Sauceboat

 Platter, 13"
Platter, 15"

 Coffeepot

 Teapot

 Warmer

 Creamer
Covered Sugar

After Dinner Cup
After Dinner Saucer

## Cupola

 Dinner Plate, 10 ½"
Salad/Dessert Plate, 8"
B & B Plate, 6 ½"
Service Plate, 12 ¼"

Cup, high
Saucer, high

Fruit, 4 ¾"

Rim Soup, 9"

Creamsoup Cup
Creamsoup Saucer

 Open Vegetable Bowl, 7"
Open Vegetable Bowl, 8 ½"
Open Vegetable Bowl, 12"

 Cov. Veget. Bowl (with feet)
Soup Tureen

Sauceboat (2 pieces)

 Platter, 12 ¼"
Platter, 14 ½"
Platter, 17"

 Coffeepot

 Teapot

 Warmer

 Creamer

 Covered Sugar

 Salt
Pepper

## Donatello

 Dinner Plate, 10"
Salad Plate, 7 ½"
B & B Plate, 6 ¾"
Service Plate (13200)

 Cup, #5 high
Saucer, #5 high

 Cup, #4 low, 7 oz.
Saucer, #4 low

 A.D. Cup, #2, 4 oz.
A.D. Saucer, #4 low

 Rim Soup, 8 ¼"

 Fruit

 Creamsoup Cup
Creamsoup Saucer

 Tureen, 90 oz.

 Covered Vegetable, 60 oz.

 Sauceboat, 13 oz.

 Open Vegetable, 66 oz.
Open Vegetable, 42 oz.

 Salt
Pepper

 Platter, 15"
Platter, 13"

 Coffeepot, #3, 47 oz.

 Teapot, #3, 44 oz.

 Sugar Bowl, #3, 9 oz.

 Creamer, #3, 8 oz.

 Cake Plate, 13"
Tort Platter

 Sandwich Tray

 Butter Dish

# Duo

Plate, flat, 26 cm
Plate, flat, 25 cm
Plate, flat, 21 cm
Plate, flat, 19 cm
Plate, flat, 15 cm
Plate, deep, 23 cm

Fruit

Creamsoup cup/saucer, 0,35 ltr.

Soup Tureen, 2,50 ltr.

Covered Vegetable Dish, 1,60 ltr.

Sauce boat (2 piece), 0,45 ltr.

Salad 3, 22 cm.
Salad 2, 20 cm.
Salad 1, 18 cm.

Pickle dish (= platter 28)

Platter rd. flat
Platter rd. deep
Platter, 38 cm.
Platter, 33 cm.
Platter, 28 cm.

Salt and Pepper

Cup/saucer 4 low, 0,25 ltr.

Cup/saucer 4 high, 0,22 ltr.
Cup/saucer 2 high, 0,10 ltr.

Coffeepot 3 (6 pers.), 1,10 ltr.
Coffeepot 2 (2 pers.), 0,70 ltr.

Teapot 4, 1,00 ltr.

Sugar bowl 3 (6 pers.), 0,20 ltr.

Creamer 3 (6 pers.), 0,21 ltr.
Creamer 2 (2 pers.), 0,11 ltr.

Cake Plate (=platter rd. flat)
Tart Platter

Sandwich tray

Butterdish

Breadbasket

Eggcup

# Flash

Dinner Plate, 10 ½"
Salad/Dessert Plate, 7 ½"
B & B Plate, 6 ¼"

Cup
Saucer

Coupe Soup, 8 ¼"

Mug

Bowl, 6"

Fruit Bowl
Bowl, 3 ½"

Bowl, 7 ½"
Bowl, 8 ¼"

Bowl, 12"

Covered Casserole/Server

Gravy Boat & Stand
Sauceboat, Small

Oblong Bowl/Baker, 12"

Fruit Bowl, 10 1/2"

Platter, 9 ½"
Platter, 14"
Platter, 17 ¼"

Fondue

Fondue Plate

Fondue Fork

Cake Plate, 14"

Carafe, 11"

Salt and Pepper Set

Coffeepot
After Dinner Coffeepot

Teapot

Tea Warmer
Coffee Warmer

Sugar
Creamer

After Dinner Cup
After Dinner Saucer

Vinegar Cruet
Oil Cruet

Egg Cup

Vase, 7"
Vase, 8 ¾"

Candleholder, 2 ¼"
Candleholder, 7 ¾"

Covered Butter Dish

# Grace

Dinner Plate, 10 ½"
Salad/Dessert Plate, 8 ½"
B & B Plate, 7"

Cup, #4 low
Saucer, #4 low

A.D. Cup
A.D. Saucer

Rim Soup

Fruit Bowl

Creamsoup Cup
Creamsoup Saucer

Soup Tureen
Covered Vegetable

Sauceboat, 2 pieces

Open Vegetable Bowl, 8"
Open Vegetable Bowl, 10"

Platter, 13"
Platter, 15"

Coffeepot

Teapot

Covered Sugar

Creamer

Salt
Pepper

# Il Faro

Dinner Plate
Salad Plate
Bread & Butter Plate
Service Plate

Cup #4 low
Saucer #4

Rim Soup
Cereal/Fruit Bowl

Cream Soup Cup
Cream Soup Saucer

Coffeepot

Teapot

Sugar Bowl (round)
Creamer (round)

Sugar Bowl (square)
Creamer (square)

Cup #4 high
Saucer #4 high

Espresso Cup #2 high
Espresso Saucer #2 high

Soup Tureen
Covered Vegetable
Sauceboat

Open Vegetable small
Open Vegetable medium
Open Vegetable large

Platter 13"
Platter 15"

Salt
Pepper

# Kaari

Plate flat, 26 cm
Plate flat, 20 cm
Plate flat, 16 cm
Plate deep, 23 cm

Fruit

Soup cup, 0,23 ltr

Vegetable dish, 2,10 ltr

Sauceboat, 0,50 ltr

Salad 3, 21 cm
Salad 2, 18 cm
Salad 1, 15 cm

Platter rd. flat, 35 cm

Platter, 38 cm
Platter, 33 cm
Platter, 24 cm

Salt and pepper

Cup 4 low, 0,20 ltr

Cup 4 high, 0,20 ltr
Cup 2 high, 0,13 ltr

Coffeepot 3, 1,45 ltr
Coffeepot 2, 0,94 ltr

Teapot 3, 1,40 ltr

Sugar 3, 0,25 ltr

Creamer 3

Butterdish

Eggcup

## Lotus

Plate flat, 25 cm
Plate flat, 21 cm
Plate flat, 19 cm
Plate flat, 17 cm
Plate deep, 21 cm
Plate deep, 19 cm

Fruit
Creamsoup cup, 0,35 ltr
Creamsoup saucer

Soup Tureen, 2,80 ltr

Covered Vegetable Dish, 1,60 ltr
Sauce Boat, 0,46 ltr

Salad 3, 21 cm
Salad 2, 19 cm
Salad 1, 17 cm

Pickle dish
Platter rd. flat

Platter, 38 cm
Platter, 33 cm
Platter, 28 cm

Salt shaker
Pepper shaker

Cup/saucer 4 low, 0,20 ltr
Cup/saucer 4 high, 0,19 ltr
Cup/saucer 2 high, 0,10 ltr

Coffeepot 3, 1,30 ltr
Coffeepot 2, 0,80 ltr

Teapot 3, 1,10 ltr

Sugar bow l 3, 0,20 ltr

Creamer/Sugar Stand, 0,18 ltr

Cake plate
Sandwich tray
Tart platter rd.

Butterdish
Eggcup

Warmer (coffee pot) 3
Warmer (coffee pot) 2

Warmer (tea pot) 3

## Magic Flute

Dinner Plate, 11"
Salad/Dessert Plate, 7 ½"
B & B Plate, 6 ¼"

Cup, #4 low
Saucer

Fruit, 5 1/8"

Creamsoup Cup
Creamsoup Saucer

Open Vegetable, Small
Open Vegetable, Medium
Open Vegetable, Large

Covered Vegetable Bowl
Stand for Covered Vegetable

Covered Sauceboat & Stand

Platter, oval 13"
Platter, oval 15"

Coffeepot
After Dinner Coffeepot

Teapot

Creamer
After Dinner Creamer

Covered Sugar
After Dinner Sugar

Stand Sugar & Creamer
Stand A.D. Sugar & Creamer

After Dinner Cup
After Dinner Saucer

## Maria

Dinner Plate, 10 ¼"
Salad Plate, 7 ½"
B & B Plate, 5 ¾"
Service Plate, 12 ¼"

Cup, #4 high, 6 oz.
Saucer, #4 high
A.D. Cup, #2 high, 2 ¾ oz.
A.D. Saucer, #2 high

Tea Cup, #4 low, 6 ¾ oz.
Saucer, #4 low

Rim Soup, 8 ¼"

Fruit, 5 ¾"

Creamsoup Cup, 9 oz.
Creamsoup Saucer

Tureen, 94 oz.

Covered Vegetable, 47 oz.

Sauceboat, 13 ½ oz., 1 pc.

Open Vegetable, #2, 48 oz.
Open Vegetable, #1, 27 oz.

Cake Plate

Sandwich Tray

Oval Platter, 15"
Oval Platter, 13"

Salt Shaker
Pepper Shaker

Coffeepot, #4, 42 oz.

Warmer

Teapot, #4, 42 oz.

Sugar Bowl, #3, 9 oz.

Creamer, #3, 6 oz.

## Monbijou

Dinner Plate, 10 ¼"
Salad Plate, 8"
B & B Plate, 6 ½"

Cup, #4 high, 7 oz.
Saucer, #4 high
A.D. Cup, #2 high, 3 ¾ oz.
A.D. Saucer, #2 high

Rim Soup, 9"

Fruit, 4 ¾"

Creamsoup Cup, 10 ¾ oz.
Creamsoup Saucer

Soup Tureen, 96 oz.

Covered Vegetable, 67 oz.

Sauceboat, 18 ½ oz., 2 pc.

Open Vegetable, #2 md., 75 oz.
Open Vegetable, #1 md., 50 oz.

Oval Platter, 15"
Oval Platter, 13"

Salt Shaker
Pepper Shaker

Coffeepot, #3, 47 oz.
A.D. Coffeepot, #2, 28 oz.

Teapot, #3, 33 oz.

Warmer

Sugar, #3, 7 oz.
Creamer, #3, 5 oz.

Covered Butter Dish

Cake Plate, 11 3/4"

Sandwich Tray

## Mythos

Place-plate, 30 cm
Plate flat, 18 cm
Plate flat, 22 cm
Plate flat, 27 cm

Plate deep, 22 cm

Fruit, 0,28 ltr

Creamsoup-cup/saucer,
0,28 ltr

Soup-tureen 2, 2,30 ltr

Covered vegetable, 1,60 ltr

Sauce-boat 2/2 pieces, 0,55 ltr

Salad 2, 1,66 ltr
Salad 3, 3,40 ltr

Pickle-dish

Platter rd. (= tart platter)

Platter, 40 cm
Platter, 50 cm

Cup/saucer 2 high, 0,09 ltr
Cup/saucer 4 high, 0,17 ltr

Cup/saucer 4 low, 0,23 ltr

Coffee-pot 3 (6 pers.), 1,20 ltr

Teapot 3, 1,30 ltr

Sugar bowl 3 (6 pers.), 0,21 ltr

Creamer 3 (6 pers.), 0,22 ltr

## Polygon

Dinner Plate, 10 ½"
Salad/Dessert Plate, 8"
B & B Plate, 6"

Cup, #5 high
Saucer*

Fruit

Rim Soup

Creamsoup Cup
Creamsoup Saucer

Open Vegetable Bowl, 7 ½"
Open Vegetable Bowl, 8 ½"

Soup Tureen

Covered Vegetable Bowl

Sauceboat (2 pieces)

Platter, 13"
Platter, 15"

Coffeepot
After Dinner Coffeepot

Teapot

Warmer

Creamer
After Dinner Creamer

Covered Sugar
After Dinner Sugar

Salt
Pepper

After Dinner Cup
After Dinner Saucer

Cake Plate

Oil Cruet, 8 ½"
Vinegar Cruet, 8 ½"

Pepper Mill, 7 ¼"

## Romance

Dinner Plate, 10 ¼"
Salad Plate, 7 ¼"
B & B Plate, 6"

Cup, #4 high
Saucer, #4
A.D. Cup, #2
A.D. Saucer, #2

Tea Cup, #4 low
Tea Saucer, #4

Coupe Soup, 7 ½"

Fruit Bowl

Creamsoup Cup
Creamsoup Saucer

Soup Tureen, 95 oz.
Covered Vegetable

Sauceboat, 18 oz.

Open Vegetable, 8"
Open Vegetable, 8 ½"

Oval Platter, 13"
Oval Platter, 15"

Salt Shaker
Pepper Shaker

Cruet

Warmer

Coffeepot
A.D. Coffeepot

Teapot

Sugar Bowl
A.D. Sugar Bowl

Creamer
A.D. Creamer

Cake Plate
Tort Tray

Sandwich Tray

Covered Butter Dish

Candleholder 6 ½"

Pitcher/Vase 6 ¾"

## Sanssouci White

Dinner Plate, 10 ¼"
Salad Plate, 7 ½"
B & B Plate, 5 ¾"
Cup, #4 low, 7 3/4 oz.
Saucer, #4 low
Cup, #4 high, 7 oz.
Saucer, #4 high
A.D. Cup, #2 high, 3 oz.
A.D. Saucer, #2 high
Rim Soup, 8 ¼"
Fruit, 5 ¾"

Creamsoup Cup, 10 ½ oz.
Creamsoup Saucer

Tureen, 132 oz.

Covered Vegetable, 50 oz.

Sauceboat, 22 oz., 1 pc.

Open Vegetable, #2, 48 oz.
Open Vegetable, #1, 27 oz.

Oval Platter, 15"
Oval Platter, 13"

Sandwich Tray

Coffeepot, #3, 37 oz.
A.D. Coffeepot, #2, 23 oz.

Teapot, #4, 42 oz.

Sugar Bowl, #3, 8 ¾ oz.
A.D. Sugar Bowl, #2, 2 ¾ oz.

Creamer, #3, 6 ½ oz.
A.D. Creamer, #2, 3 oz.

Cake Plate with Handles

Tort Tray

Covered Butter Dish

Fruit/Bread Basket

## Scenario

Dinner Plate
Salad
Service Plate

Cup #4, high
Saucer

Soup

Fruit

Bowl, 4"

Soup Tureen

Covered Vegetable

Cheese Platter

Open Vegetable Bowl, Small
Open Vegetable Bowl, Medium
Open Vegetable Bowl, Large

Sauceboat

Platter, 10 ¾"
Platter, 15"
Platter, Deep, 13 ¾"

Coffeepot

Creamer

Covered Sugar

Salt
Pepper

Covered Butter

After Dinner Cup
After Dinner Saucer

Beer Stein/Mug, Small
Beer Stein, Large

Covered Box

Ashtray

Salt/Pepper Gift Box

Oil/Vinegar

# Suomi

Dinner Plate, 10 ¼"
Salad/Dessert Plate, 8"
B & B Plate, 6 ¼"

Service Plate, 11"
Cake Plate

Cup, #4, low
Saucer

Fruit

Rim Soup

Creamsoup Cup
Creamsoup Saucer

Open Vegetable, Small
Open Vegetable, Medium
Open Vegetable, Large

Covered Vegetable Bowl
(3 pieces)

Covered Sauceboat and
Stand (4 pieces)

Platter, 13" Rectangular
Platter, 15" Rectangular

Coffeepot
After Dinner Coffeepot

Teapot

Warmer

Covered Creamer (2 pieces)
Covered Sugar

Salt
Pepper

After Dinner Cup
After Dinner Saucer

# Variation

Plate flat, 26 cm, 25 cm, 21
cm, 19 cm, 17 cm, 15 cm

Plate deep, 23 cm

Fruit/Soup cup/
saucer, with stand, 0,30 ltr

Soup tureen 2
with stand, 2,65 ltr
Soup tureen 2, 2,65 ltr

Cov. veg. dish
and stand, 1,65 ltr
Covered vegetable dish, 1,65 ltr

Stand for tureen
Stand for covered vegetable dish

Sauceboat 2/2 piece, 0,40 ltr

Salad 2, 22 cm
Salad 1, 18 cm

Pickle dish
= platter, 28 cm

Platter rd. flat
(= cake plate)

Platter, 38 cm
Platter, 33 cm
Platter, 28 cm

Salt and pepper

Cup & saucer 4 l, 0,22 ltr

Cup & saucer 4 h, 0,18 ltr
Cup & saucer 2 h, 0,09 ltr

Coffeepot 3, 1,20 ltr
Coffeepot 2, 0,65 ltr

Teapot 4, 1,10 ltr

Sugar 3, 0,22 ltr
Sugar 2, 0,12 ltr

Creamer 3
Creamer 2

Cake plate

Sandwich tray

Butterdish

Jam dish

Eggcup

# Cutlery Shapes

### Asymmetria

Table Fork    Table Spoon    Table Knife    Dessert Fork    Tea Spoon    Soup Ladle    Sauce Ladle    Serving Spoon    Serving Fork    Meat Fork    Pie Server

### Composition

Table Fork    Table Knife    Table Spoon    Salad/Dessert Fork    Tea Spoon    Gravy Ladle    Meat Fork    Serving Spoon    Serving Fork

### Concav

Table Spoon    Table Fork    Table Knife    Salad Fork    Tea Spoon    Serving Spoon    Soup Ladle    Gravy Ladle    Meat Fork    Serving Fork    Cake Server

## Dialog

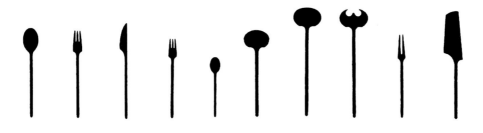

Table Spoon   Table Fork   Table Knife   Salad Fork   Tea Spoon   Sauce Ladle   Serving Spoon   Serving Fork   Meat Fork   Pie Server

## Giro

Table Spoon   Table Fork   Table Knife   Salad Fork   Tea Spoon   Soup Ladle   Gravy Ladle   Serving Spoon   Serving Fork   Meat Fork   Cake Server

## Sculptura

Table Spoon   Table Fork   Table Knife   Salad Fork   Tea Spoon   Sauce Ladle   Serving Spoon   Serving Fork   Meat Fork   Pie Server   Espresso Spoon

202

## String

Table Fork　Salad Fork　Soup Ladle　Serving Spoon　Meat Fork

Table Spoon　Table Knife　Tea Spoon　Gravy Ladle　Serving Fork　Cake Server

## Suomi

Table Fork　Dessert Fork　Gravy Ladle　Serving Fork　Pie Server

Table Spoon　Table Knife　Tea Spoon　Serving Spoon　Meat Fork

## Taille

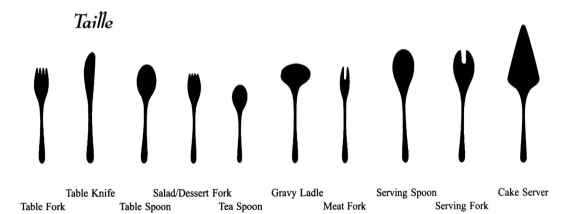

Table Knife　Salad/Dessert Fork　Gravy Ladle　Serving Spoon　Cake Server

Table Fork　Table Spoon　Tea Spoon　Meat Fork　Serving Fork

# Bibliography

Brohan, Torsten, and Thomas Berg. *Avantgarde Design 1880-1930*. Edited by Simone Philippi. Germany: Benedikt Tashen, 1994.

*Design Since 1945*. Philadelphia Museum of Art, 1983.

Eidelberg, Martin, ed. *Design 1935-1965, What Modern Was*. New York: Harry Abrams, Inc., 1991.

Garner, Philippe, ed. *Encyclopedia of Decorative Arts 1890-1940*. New York: Van Nostrand Reinhold, 1978.

Lucie-Smith, Edward. *Industrial Design*. New York: Van Nostrand Reinhold, 1983.

Opie, Jennifer Hawkins, ed. *Scandinavia Ceramics and Glass in the Twentieth Century*. Collections of the Victoria and Albert Museum. New York: Rizzoli International Publications, 1989.

In addition, much historical information has been found in the *Studio Year Books*, now out of print and circulation, and many phone conversations over a fifteen year period with past and present American Sales Representatives have contributed to the exactness of the information presented in this book.

# Notes